SAVE
YOUR
LICENSE

SAVE YOUR LICENSE

A DRIVER'S SURVIVAL GUIDE

by Gene Mason

Legal counsel by William R. Gray

Illustrations by Thomas Myers

Library of Congress Cataloging in Publication Data:

Mason, Gene W. 1928-
    SAVE YOUR LICENSE: A Driver's Survival Guide.

    1. Speed limits — United States. 2. Automobile drivers' licenses — United States. 3. Automobile driving — United States. I. Title.
HE5620.S6M37   388.3'14   78-2218
ISBN 0-87364-103-5

Printed in the United States of America.

PALADIN press

Post Office Box 1307
Boulder, Colorado 80306

This book is dedicated to man and justice

may they soon find one another.

TABLE OF CONTENTS

Introduction

This is a book about driving and about freedom.

America, like no other country, has been the proud land of the automobile. There are more makes, more accessories, more interest, and just plain more autos than anywhere else on earth. Every month thousands of books and magazines are sold with information on obtaining more power and speed from your automobile. Some also have articles on increasing highway safety and performance through better brakes and suspension, and a few discuss vehicle handling during high speed maneuvers. Nearly every city of substantial size has "high performance shops" dispensing a variety of accessories. Several excellent driving schools are in operation to train drivers in the elements of high speed maneuvering and control. But — after absorbing and/or acquiring this material, how can you keep the flashing (red, more recently blue) light from appearing in your rear view mirror, as happened to some thirty million motorists last year?

America, while still the champion of freedom, has had a considerable erosion in this area through the years. The writers and publisher of this book are advocating individual freedoms, but not license. None of us has any quarrel with necessary police capabilities of command, control and apprehension. But, the fifty-five mile per hour speed limit was dictated to U.S. drivers by an oil cartel, and has been converted into a revenue producing device in too many localities. In the name of traffic safety, well-paid armed men in high speed cars lie in wait along our highways, using expensive radar and radio nets to snare drivers who would not have been speeding a few years ago. Three times as many speeding citations are issued now as during the seventy mile per hour days.

Some readers may question the need and propriety of a textbook of ticket-evading tactics. In this writer's opinion, the number of defensive measures available indicates the basic imperfection of present traffic controls. It is doctrine in all schools of law that the system must constantly be tested. If a public law, after an enormous effort, is still ineffective at controlling citable offenses, perhaps the trouble lies with the basis of the law itself, and not, as is suggested by some, with a shortage of patrols or radar sets. It would seem, in particular, that it is past time to stop the morally bankrupt practice of victimizing the driving public in order to raise traffic fines as revenue.

Such fines could be called illegal taxes, because in the morass of the nation's conflicting traffic laws, there is no way to avoid being in technical violation regularly. Certain bureaucrats, knowing this, have experimented with robot cameras, citing secretly, and then mailing coercive demands for fines to our homes. Beware of this line of thought . . . it can lead to a national traffic police system of sinister power and proportions.

It is my contention that alert high-speed driving is not necessarily dangerous, and that frequently the most dangerous motorists are ignored by the police. How many times have you seen a traffic-blocking motorist doing thirty miles per hour in a fifty-five mile per hour zone with no penalty, while you were cited for doing sixty or seventy miles per hour in the same zone? Much of the information commonly quoted to you relating speed to highway accidents and fatalities is speculative at best, and often more fictive than factual. This books begins by documenting some of those distortions and discrepancies.

Many of last year's thirty million traffic tickets were issued to motorists in excellent control of automobiles designed for safe high-speed driving on highways constructed for safe high-speed driving. This book was written for them. With highway justice often haphazard at best, perhaps these chapters will help even the score, while at the same time accentuating highway alertness.

Since technology is available to all in this country, we have countervailing measures available to us as private drivers. Citizens band channels, radar detectors, police band scanners, as well as legal strategems, are all advocated and described in detail in this book. We feel that any device which makes an officer's presence known — even a warning from one speeder to another — contributes to public order. But, there are individual "public safety departments" that seem to prefer to have their traffic surveillance kept secret from the populace. They would take away your access to air waves, confiscate your radar detector and scanner. As of this writing, Connecticut, Virginia and several cities continue their prosecution of radar detector owners, while other states are considering similar bans.

Those of us who assembled this book like to think that the driver who takes the time to read and use this book is a knowledgeable motorist who takes pride in a safe, well-equipped car. He or she is part of the solution to the need for efficient, enjoyable driving, not part of the growing problem.

I would like to thank Peder Lund — publisher, editor, and kindred soul — for having the courage to undertake the publication of a book of this character. I thankfully credit Whit Collins with his contributions to the researching of citizen band radio and police scanners, and extend my gratitude to Chrysler, Ford, General Motors, Kustom Signals, and Electrolert for providing me with some of the research material. In addition, I would like to thank various state and municipal police for their cooperation, however unwitting.

Chapter I
The Case for Speed

We open this chapter with two questions. First: would a passenger be safer cruising down the highway at eighty miles per hour in a new, $15,000 sports car with Parnelli Jones at the wheel; or traveling the same road at the legal speed limit of fifty-five miles per hour in an unsound automobile of 1953 vintage, operated by an incompetent driver? If you picked the incompetent, this book is not for you, and you might as well put it back on the shelf. Otherwise, read on.

Second question: Who do you think the police would ticket? Parnelli Jones! Get my point? No consideration is made for the age, experience, physical condition or intelligence of the driver, nor for the condition of his automobile. Why is the speed limit the same for a dilapidated car ten to twenty years old, with poor suspension, brakes, and tires, as for a new sports car designed for safe high speed? One cannot assume all cars to be equally safe. Perhaps one could argue that it would be difficult to enforce different speed limits for different cars and/or drivers, but would this not imply that justice is too much to expect from our law officers and legal system?

Let us go further. If you often have the feeling that you may be exceeding the speed limit while keeping pace with the traffic flow, you are probably right. In 1968 the U.S. Bureau of Public Roads collected speed data on level, straight sections of main highways, including the Interstate System, during off-peak periods of the day when traffic densities were low, and drivers were traveling at their desired speeds. The investigators found that when the speed limit was sixty miles per hour, forty-five percent of the vehicles were traveling faster; when the limit was fifty miles per hour, eighty-one percent were traveling faster; and when the posted limit was forty miles per hour, an astounding ninety-seven percent were traveling faster than the specified limit. The results of another study show that eighty-five percent of all traffic in a given situation operates at a reasonable speed, regardless of the posted limit. In 1976 the State Highways Department monitored traffic at thirty-five locations across the State of Washington, and found that fifty-two percent were cruising in excess of fifty-five miles per hour.

This departure from the speed limit increased in 1977. According to a recent U.S. Transportation Department study, sixty-two percent of the vehicles in Washington now exceed the limit. But that is nothing compared to Wyoming and Connecticut where seventy-seven percent exceed the fifty-five mile per hour limit. (It is interesting what little, if any, impact the banning of radar detectors has had in Connecticut). In fact, the closest compliance to the fifty-five mile per hour limit in the country is Virginia, where thirty percent still exceed the limit.

Let us examine the safety aspects a bit more in depth before moving on, in case you are not convinced. Consider, for example, what was happening on the roads before the fifty-five mile per hour limit. In 1971, Maine and Vermont had two of the slowest highway limits in the country: forty-five miles per hour and fifty miles per hour, respectively. The motor vehicle death rate per capita for both states was 0.029. The District of Columbia, on the other hand, which had no highway speed limit (reasonable and proper), had a vehicle death date per capita of .017, or about forty percent lower. During the same year, Kansas, Iowa, Texas, and Colorado had highway limits of seventy miles per hour, with about the same death rate per capita as Maine and Vermont.

At this point, you may be saying, "Hey, wait a minute. You should be comparing highway fatalities per mile driven, not per area population." All right. During the same period, Vermont, with a speed limit of fifty miles per hour, had a death rate of 6.7 per one hundred million vehicle miles. This rate exceeded those of Colorado (5.1), Iowa (5.0), Montana (6.0), South Dakota (5.9), Texas (5.7) and Kansas (4.3), all with speed limits of seventy miles per hour. Maine, with a speed limit of forty-five miles per hour, had a death rate of 4.9 per one hundred million vehicles miles, a rate higher than that of Kansas, although Kansas had a speed limit of seventy miles per hour. All this is not to say that the absence of a speed limit means fewer highway deaths, but it does indicate that there is no clean-cut relationship between posted speed limits and highway fatalities.

Still have lingering doubts? Maybe we should look at some data collected after the enactment of the fifty-five miles per hour limit, which took place in 1974. In 1973, during the busy driving month of June (according to statistics provided by the Washington State Office of Program Planning and Fiscal Management, Information Services Division), we find 3.15 deaths per 100 million vehicle miles, as opposed to 3.71 deaths in June 1974. This is especially significant in view of the fact that there were 91,856 motor vehicles registered in 1973, and only 77,391 registered in 1974.

If you want to look at the whole year, here it is. Recently released statistics from the Records Section, Washington State Patrol, entitled "1974 Washington Motor Vehicle Fatal Traffic Collision Summary," indicate that fatal collisions increased in 1974, the first year of the new law, to 668 from 656 in 1973, despite a decreasing trend during preceding years. The most dramatic drop ever in traffic deaths in Washington occured in 1973, when the freeway limit was still a reasonable seventy miles per hour. In 1976 the fifty-five miles per hour "safe limit" registered 819 highway fatalities.

The Comptroller General of the United States, in a report to Congress dated February 17, 1977, indicated that our fifty-five mile per hour limit is a failure. Part of the report states: "Oregon State Police have analyzed this resource allocation problem in some detail. In terms of highway emphasis, Oregon State Police devote about one third of their traffic patrol time to freeways, but only six percent of Oregon traffic fatalities are occurring on the freeways. This leaves the other roads, on which ninety-four percent of fatalities occur, a proportionately smaller patrol coverage. In terms of traffic-enforcement emphasis, fifty-three percent of total traffic arrests have been for speeds over fifty-five miles per hour. However, only five percent of the driving errors in Oregon's fatal accidents have been attributed to excessive speed that may or may not have been over fifty-five miles per hour.

"Oregon State Police believe that spending so much time on the enforcement of one law has affected the enforcement of other accident-causing violations. For example, twenty percent of the driving errors in Oregon's fatal accidents were for being on the wrong side of the highway, but this violation has received proportionately less emphasis than speeds over fifty-five miles per hour.

"Some state officials said that the states have been given the responsibility for enforcing an unpopular law. These factors have contributed to a loss of morale and prestige among enforcement personnel and to the growing disrespect for laws and law enforcement officials."

Lee N. Hames, Director of Safety Education for the American Medical Association states that "the new fifty-five mile per hour speed limit has been given undue credit for a reduction in highway fatalities. Most crashes occur at speeds of less than fifty-five miles per hour anyway. We hope, of course, that the nationwide trend continues, but we believe that the savings in lives cannot honestly be attributed to any great extent to the reduction in the speed limit.

"It seems dubious that drinking drivers who are involved in so many fatal crashes will be too influenced by lower speed limits, since they already are disobeying the law by driving while intoxicated. And we don't see much change in the number of drunken pedestrians who are killed each year."

If speed is not the big culprit, then what is? James Wilson, Associate Administrator of the Department of Transportation's National Highway Traffic Safety Administration, points out that almost three percent of American drivers are alcoholics, and another four percent are heavy escape drinkers. Studies made over a period of years show that alcohol contributes to between fifty and sixty percent of all traffic fatalities.

Walt Woron, columnist for Competition Press and Autoweek, asks a frightening question. "Every time you drive between the hours of 6 p.m. and early morning, did you realize every twenty-fifth driver you meet is 'legally drunk?'" (The term "legally drunk" is used here to indicate a blood alcohol concentration of .10 percent or more).

A certain percentage of accidents also result from drug use, physical abnormalities and mental disturbances. Some experts have speculated that as many as fifteen percent of all fatal accidents may be suicides.

We find it particularly interesting that several years ago the National Highway Traffic Safety Administration established a realistic goal of a one third reduction in traffic fatalities, with no consideration of reducing the speed limit. They have already come a long way toward this goal by improving highways (the Interstate Highway System is approximately twice as safe as the rest of the nation's highways), and by setting safe vehicle standards. During the period when all the credit for decreasing the national highway death toll was going to speed reduction, the following automobile safety improvements were being suggested, and some were being acted upon and enforced by private industry and various governmental organizations:

Improved brake standards.
Decreased flammability of interior materials.
Increased protection from roof collapse.

Child safety seating systems.

Extension of requirements for seats and seat belts in trucks and buses.

Improved safety qualities of side and rear windows.

Improved interior impact protection (padding).

Improved protection of driver from steering assembly.

Rear underride protection.

Improved fuel system integrity (fire protection).

Improved side door strength.

One might also consider that the speed limit is the same whether the road is dry, wet or icy. Some roads do have an allowance made for night over day, but most do not.

I recall being stopped on a deserted stretch of freeway early one bright Sunday morning for driving ten miles per hour over the speed limit. I asked the officer if he could see anything unsafe about my speed, or the way I controlled my vehicle. "No," came the expected answer, "but you were exceeding the posted limit." I received a ticket, and the following week the speed limit in that area was increased by ten miles per hour. What was a crime one week was not a crime the next, but I never heard of anyone receiving a refund.

You will also notice that speed limits on similar roads differ from state to state, and that sometimes the speed limits are the same on roads of vastly differing accident potential. Apparently, what is safe in one state is not safe in another, and the back country road with no shoulders is as safe as the freeway. Of course, the truth of the matter is that speed limits are largely arbitrary rules with few, if any, scientific principles involved.

It would, perhaps, be cynical to mention that five to ten percent of most city budgets are financed by traffic fines. In fact, if the revenue from traffic fines received by the municipalities of the State of Washington is divided by the number of people in those cities, the average revenue from each person comes out an astounding five dollars per year. This is the state average — some cities have individual averages as high as fifty dollars per person per year! Applying the same method to county revenues in the state, one arrives at a yearly average of four dollars per person. Most people live in both a city and a county; the combined yearly revenue averages nine dollars per person in additional "taxes."

Since the above figures do not include interstate highway fines, we will look into that area. In 1975, the State of Washington collected $21.4 million in traffic fines of which seventy-five to eighty percent was for speeding violations.

And — of course, there are always the particular noteworthies.

Strangely, there must be a terrible wave of traffic "crime" in little Willow Springs, Illinois (population 3,300), since they raked in $200,000 in traffic fines from trucks and cars in 1976. However, that is meager compared to the 1977 two-month haul of $63,400 in speeding tickets by the 1000 population of Lauderdale-by-the-Sea, Florida. All in the interest of safety, naturally.

The courts and traffic departments maintain that such revenue collection is necessary to curb offenders, but is this really true? The U.S. Department of Transportation has just issued the results of a three-year pilot program, begun in 1973 by the Seattle Municipal Court and the Washington State Department of Motor Vehicles. The study revealed that traffic law violators who receive heavy fines are more likely to become repeat offenders. Drivers who paid smaller traffic fines on citations had fewer repeat violations, perhaps because they were "reciprocating for lower fines with safer driving."

Some will contend that driving at lower speeds is important in order to conserve energy. The difficulty with this argument is that the speeding ticket is issued by the arresting officer ordinarily charges the driver not with energy waste, but with unsafe speed, thereby jeopardizing his driver's license, increasing his insurance rates, and treating him as a criminal. In the interest of justice, it should be mentioned that a few states (Montana and Idaho, for example — there may be others) have laws allowing the issuance of tickets for energy wasting by automobiles traveling between fifty-five and seventy miles per hour. These are subject to a fine of a few dollars and are not recorded on the driving record.

If we limit the argument to energy alone, however, we still find several faults in the concept. It is well known that all kinds of sleek, efficient small cars are getting better fuel mileage at seventy miles per hour than are heavy sedans cruising at forty-five miles per hour. Trucks, because of gearing in relation to engine revolutions, also usually get better mileage at higher speeds. As a matter of record, The Federal Energy Administration Office admits that in 1973 American drivers used a daily average of 263 million gallons of gasoline. In 1974, after the lower limit was imposed, daily gas consumption averaged 271 million gallons. In 1975 the figure climbed to 281 million gallons.

Since there are few repressive speed limits in Europe, does that mean there is no oil shortage there? Well — all of us know Europeans have less petroleum than we do, but perhaps they have a more enlightened attitude in some areas than we do. The U.S. has the most well-developed road system in the world, far more impressive than West Germany's Autobahns, France's Autoroutes, or Italy's

Autostadi. The Europeans think our speed limit is a monstrous joke. Oh — to be honest, I should mention that last year the Italians announced a national speed limit of eighty miles per hour. I understand that this constitutes a real hardship on Italian drivers.

As to what is wrong with a fifty-five mile per hour limit — Well, besides the fact that there is no evidence to show that it decreases fatalities, is not always fuel saving, and wastes enormous amounts of time, there is good evidence to show that it promotes a disregard for the law. Our interstates were designed for speeds in the range of seventy miles per hour, and the public knows it. Present surveys show that average interstate traffic is cruising along at sixty-five miles per hour, not fifty-five miles per hour. The present limit has tended to reduce respect for state highway patrolmen, while at the same time perhaps increasing ulcers, tension headaches, stress coronaries, and maybe even increased accidents from falling asleep while succumbing to the hypnotic boredom of fifty-five.

Dr. Ronald S. Morris of Texas A & M recently presented a paper on a noteworthy experiment at a meeting of the SAFE Association, an organization of safety equipment researchers, manufacturers, and users. He attempted to scientifically establish the "comfortable" freeway speed for an average driver in an average vehicle on a dry, sunny, day. He used a 1970 Datsun 240 Z, a 1973 Ford Torino station wagon, and a GMC Sports Van, and employed eighteen volunteers. Each was told that he was participating in an experiment intended to measure various human factors associated with driving. In each vehicle, the speedometer was masked and the driver did not know his speed was being measured and recorded. Each driver was asked to find a speed which was comfortable and to maintain it. The analysis of the data "resulted in an overall mean comfortable speed of 69.94 miles per hour with a standard deviation of 4.425 miles per hour. From this it is reasonable to conclude that the probability that the entire population's comfortable speed is 55 miles per hour is essentially zero. The net effect of this mismatch them will be increased control effort by the driver and consequently increased fatigue," he said. "Further, any relaxation of constant vigilance by the driver will result in a tendency to return to the comfortable speed. Further, the constant throttle correction will result in poor engine performance and efficiency . . ."

The experiment did reveal some variance in comfort speed in different vehicles, with "mean velocities of 66 miles per hour for the station wagon, 70 miles per hour for the sports car, and 77 miles per hour for the van.

"The comfortable speed demonstrates that if the present speed limit of 55 miles per hour is to be continued, further research is needed in the areas of vehicle and roadway design to establish a more acceptable interface between inherent vehicle characteristics and legal speed limits," Morris concluded. "If the difference between the comfortable speed and the legal speed is large, the driver is placed in a stressful and fatiguing situation. This additional stress can lead to exposure to greater accident hazard."

There is an additional problem with speed limits in some states (Colorado, Idaho, Louisiana, Maryland, New Hampshire, New Mexico, Rhode Island, South Dakota, and Texas). These states have what are known as prima facie limits. This is perhaps one of the biggest travesties of justice. A prima facie limit states that any speed in excess of an arbitrary standard established by the state (this differs in different states) is automatically considered reckless driving. This concept has sweeping implications. For example, a driver in Rhode Island doing over forty-five miles per hour at night or fifty miles per hour in the daytime, hardly frantic speeds, is considered driving recklessly by the law. If at that modest speed he were involved in an accident, even though it would not be considered his fault by any unbiased observer, he would be guilty of contributory negligence at least, and possibly gross negligence. He could be required to pay accident victims not only heavy personal damages, but punitive damages as well, because gross negligence is a criminal charge. In the event of a death he could be charged with voluntary manslaughter, carrying a penalty of fifteen years in some states.

While we are about it, let us see how fairly the traffic police play the game. While it is a well-known fact that the sight of a police car deters violators of all kinds, many states will persist in using unmarked police cars, not to prevent violations, but to support revenues. I once saw a police car with a ski rack mingling with homeward bound skiers, hoping for a catch. More than once I have been followed uncomfortably close by a car pushing me to widen the gap, only to find it was a plain wrapper bear looking for a meal.

Recently a friend of mine was stopped by the state police on a freeway. The officer's complaint was lodged in the form of a question. "Do you know that for the last eight miles you have been going fifty-seven miles per hour?" This happened the very same day I read a newspaper plea for a larger state budget to increase the number of state patrol cars. This article was nestled between accounts of serious crimes. Makes one wonder what the government considers top priorities.

Although most traffic patrolmen deny it, many divisions still have a required quota of tickets to issue. For instance, the Seattle Police

Department openly admits that for many years they have set an "informal" requirement that each officer issue at least one citation per shift, and that the policy be "one measure of an officer's work performance." Supervisors have been known to tell their patrolmen that if they did not issue a ticket a day for each day in the month, they would be expected to issue two a day the following month. I need not point out that such policies result in unwarranted tickets, infuriate the citizenry, and cause a loss of respect for police officers. I suspected that I was a victim of such a policy once when I received a ticket for going forty-two miles per hour in a forty mile per hour zone. Can a police speedometer be that accurate, let alone judge another car's speed by that margin? Absurd.

And finally — if you think you have legal recourse to question the judgment or integrity of the arresting officer, think again. For all practical purposes you are judged, convicted, and sentenced at the scene. It is rare indeed for the average citizen to be able to convince a judge in his favor over a patrolman, even if he felt he could afford the time and the legal expense. This is especially true if the judge is a justice of the peace, who in many cases may share some of the fine. Talk about conflict of interest!

Chapter II
On Being Insignificant

One of the basic principles in avoiding the bears is to avoid the appearance of speed. Keeping a low profile is essential; certain vehicles look as if they are going very fast, even at slow speeds. Years ago I owned one of the first E-type Jaguars, and nearly ran the risk of receiving a speeding ticket while parked. Sports and other cars fairly reeking of go power invite tickets. Ever notice that most Corvettes move surprisingly slowly? Many Corvette drivers are just plain ticket wary and weary. I remember driving an Austin-Healey within the speed limit, past a parked police car. The officer immediately hit the flashing light and took off after me. I pulled over, and he examined my driver's license. He then apologetically explained that when I drove by he was sure that I was speeding, but when he matched my speed, he discovered that I was not. Unfortunately, most police would not admit their error and lose face in that manner.

While it is a well known psychological fact that certain colors have a tendency to generate certain emotions, we think it is a bit specious to give this factor much consideration with respect to automobile colors. There is also no question, however, that certain colors are more clearly visible and attract more attention than others. If you add racing strips, psychedelic touches or offbeat two-tones, watch out.

I have more than one friend who has received all his speeding tickets in his sports car, although he drives the family sedan in the same manner. All of which illustrates the fact that if you drive something that looks fast, you are going to have to be even more alert for

15

Smokey Bear. Incidentally, one of the best examples of insignificant looks with high performance potential is the unmarked police car, which we will discuss in a later chapter.

There is, of course, another way of attracting unnecessary attention from the bears — have some element of illegality about your vehicle. This can be the absence of a current license plate or safety sticker (where required), a burned-out headlight or tail light, or noisy muffler. A poorly illuminated license plate seems to be a favorite target. Most states require the rear plate to be properly lit, and broken or burned-out bulbs in this location are common. I have been stopped, purportedly for lack of mud-flaps on the rear of my dune-buggy, although this was obviously a ploy to check the vehicle for any other possible defects.

There is a little trick I have found extremely helpful in those situations when I have just inadvertently bombed past a police car which was parked or approaching down a side road. To flash your brake lights is like announcing that you were speeding but saw the police car. Chances are you will buy yourself a ticket that way. Under these circumstances, my strategy goes like this: I ease off the gas pedal and grab the emergency brake for several quick pulls, and my car slows. The bears see no brake light, match up speeds, realize I am not speeding, and turn off.

The police most commonly spot speeders by comparing speeds of vehicles on the road, frequently choosing a high vantage point (usually an overpass or a place high on a freeway entry ramp) from which to observe traffic flow. The speeder below stands out from the pack and so is easy to isolate. The cop slips in behind him and makes the speed determination by pacing (standard or moving radar) or by VASCAR. An officer once told me, "I estimate that the car you passed was slightly exceeding the speed limit, and you made him look like he was parked." That unfortunate incident occurred a week before an important race. I had just fine tuned my sports car and was taking it for a trial run on a strip of divided highway with no intersections. The car I passed was the only one on the road except for that of the policeman, which I did not see, parked at a weighing station across the parkway or median strip. Our rather unpleasant conversation took place some fifteen miles from the scene of the crime, after I had stopped to do a little further tuning. All I can say is that he was definitely a super sorehead.

The lesson here is that you should move slowly through a pack of freeway cars, in case you are being observed. Pick up speed to the next pack, slowly move through it, and then speed on to the next. Cars usually do travel in such groups.

16

The police seldom expect a car to speed uphill, primarily because they know that most drivers maintain a given accelerator pressure while cruising and slow down while ascending. Besides, most cars are not capable of speeding up a hill unless they approach it at great speed. Consequently, one rarely finds the cops clocking around hills. An added benefit to you is that you can slow in a very short distance while traveling uphill. This used to play an important role when I was competing in automobile hillclimbs on mountain roads. But let me add one word of caution. While police are not likely to have radar set up on a hill, a police car some distance behind has a particularly good view of your ascent for comparison speeds if there are other cars. So, slow down as you near the crest, until you know who is back there closing on you, or what is ahead.

Although it is illegal to exceed the speed limit even when passing another vehicle, most police will allow brief spurts of speed as long as you quickly return to the limit, because they cannot clock you that quickly. This can occasionally be used to advantage, even when you know the police may be nearby.

Certainly one of the best ways to avoid the police while you are moving rapidly from here to there is to find a speedy sucker to follow. Nine times out of ten the police will stop only the lead car. If he stops or turns off, you can slow a bit and wait for another leader to overtake you. There are several considerations to keep in mind, though. You must place enough space between the two of you so that the officer does not pick you both up for racing. And it is equally important to follow closely enough so that it is clear that you are following a pace set by another car. If you drop back too far, the officer may spot only you. I have found that about a hundred yards is usually right. This technique is somewhat limited. If the leader is cruising at 90 to 100 miles per hour, for example, you are pretty obviously aware of the speed, and could have difficulty passing it off as simply unwittingly following a pace. It is best accomplished at 10 to 15 miles per hour over the limit. Occasionally the vehicle I pick to follow is a police car. Sometimes they cruise at speeds considerably over the limit, especially county or sheriff's patrol cars. The law does not permit them or any other vehicle to exceed the speed limit unless a flashing light and/or a siren is used, so they can be followed if they are not using such equipment. How could you be more righteous than by following an example set by a minion of the law?

There are a few other stunts sometimes used that I have saved for last because of their rather dubious value. One theory is that if you cruise fast enough, say at speeds in excess of ninety miles per hour, you will avoid the police because none will routinely overtake you

17

On Being Insignificant

correct

incorrect

while patrolling the highway or even in a sweep, and a few may not choose to chase you at that speed. Granted, none is likely to routinely overtake you, but this system does not allow for the bears lying in wait, and most police equipment is designed for a good chase. Another possibility is finding a roadblock ultimately waiting for you, since you cannot outspeed radio waves. This happened to an internationally known Grand Prix driver, an acquaintance of mine.

It would be a good idea to mention at this point that many states have a few hours, usually the two to five range in the early morning, when there are almost no police on the highway. In fact, my state for many years had a few hours with *no* highway patrol, except on call for emergencies. Such information can be valuable, but usually is fairly difficult to dig out.

Another unreliable method of avoiding the police is to speed only on the right, normally slower, lane of a freeway, the idea being that the police are watching the left, or passing lane, for speeders. This practice has its limitations. If there is no traffic, it will not matter where you speed if the cops are watching, and if traffic is heavy, this technique requires a lot of lane shifting, which is one of the things police look for. However, this ploy can be of value for short stretches where the right lanes are clear. Radar speed meters usually direct the beam down all approaching freeway lanes, so where these meters are in use you are safer on the right only if there are vehicles ahead of you for blocking purposes.

Finally, I would like to recommend that whenever you pass another vehicle you leave your turn signal blinking a bit longer than you ordinarily would. The bears watch for quick or clumsy maneuvers, and from a distance this technique will give the impression that the passing was done in a leisurely fashion. This is rather like the opera singer who leaves his mouth open for a brief period of time after a note is finished to create an illusion of greater endurance.

Chapter III
Speed Detection Systems

A multitude of techniques have been used by the police to detect vehicles exceeding the speed limits. Basically, these are: pacing, visual clocking, the hose, Orbis, VASCAR, and radar. Some of these systems are still very much in use, and some have been virtually abandoned. We should mention that the California Highway Patrol does not use radar at all. In spite of this handicap, they managed to issue 1.2 million speeding tickets last year using alternate techniques. Since radar is currently the most common nationally used method and the most complex, we have devoted another chapter to its consideration.

Pacing

If you have been on the road for many years, you remember when all you had to watch for was the well-marked highway patrol car slipping up on you and approaching closely enough to match your speed to determine whether you were speeding. In recent years the unmarked police car has complicated the vigilance, but the technique is still common. A cop may, of course, employ a variety of methods to sneak up on you, using your blind spot, or appearing suddenly from an entrance.

A modification of pacing is the so-called sweep. This tactic is still in use in most states. When many drivers exceed the posted speed limit, as they do today, most state highway patrols issue standing orders to pick off the leaders. An officer will approach clumps of cars at relatively high speed, say sixty-five to seventy miles per hour. Of those that he does not immediately pass, he tickets the leaders, perhaps having to weave through traffic to do so. The patrol authorities usually dismiss the resulting hazard to surrounding cars by citing the officers' superior driving skills and well-equipped patrol cars. The hazards of chase-pace driving are also used to excuse the purchase by the police departments of expensive radar speed detectors.

Visual Clocking

These methods are often facilitated by white marking bands placed across highways to denote one eighth or quarter mile distances, and are quite common in some states. Sometimes, municipalities mark off 100 yard portions of city streets for the same reason.

An officer, usually equipped with a stop watch, will be stationed at an overpass or by a crossroads, or perhaps at the top of an entrance ramp. He may also be on a highway median, near a turnaround. Smokey will always be at a vantage point, with rapid access to the road. He can also follow you by car, clicking his stop watch as you pass over the marker strips. Timing you in this manner is very similar to the VASCAR following mode discussed in a subsequent section.

In much the same way, police helicopters or fixed-wing aircraft can scan drivers as they cross the white bands. The police fixed-wing planes are invariably single-engine high-winged craft, used for better visibility of the ground below. The bear in the air can also use landmarks of known distances to one another, but the white highway bands are by far the most convenient method for any form of clocking. Watch out for these bands at all times. Slowing down or stopping between them can frustrate the system.

There are numerous drawbacks to clocking by aircraft and radioing the results to a highway patrol car, and that old devil expense is probably foremost. It can cost over $100 an hour to keep a helicopter up. Light aircraft are much cheaper, but in some states the pilot-officer who timed the violator must land to sign the ticket prepared by the patrol car officer who makes the apprehension. Helicopters have that capability, but fixed-wing aircraft do not. Bear in mind that no aircraft can use the VASCAR system, because there is no road odometer to key into a computer. Therefore, all observations must be man-made marks or other reference points as close to the traveled portion of the highway as possible. Questions of visual distortion can defeat an eye in the sky citation. During certain high traffic periods of the year, authorities are most prone to use helicopters for traffic patrol, partly because these aircraft are so obvious. At other times, the expense of aircraft, pilot, chase car and highway

21

patrol personnel — four officers are sometimes required to award one air ticket — is deemed too high.

The Hose

Flashing headlights used to be our primary means of signalling that there were traffic cops ahead, often warning that a hose trap was operating nearby.

The guts of this system consisted of two relatively inconspicious gray hoses placed sixteen feet apart. Using the same pneumatic principle as a service station yard bell, the hoses tripped an electronic tube-type counter chronograph that reads speeds off to a waiting highway patrol officer, who would then radio to a chase car stationed where it could quickly apprehend the speeder.

Ironically, the officers' dislike of the setup chores and boring vigils contributed to the disuse of the hose traps. Setting up operations ordinarily required two patrolmen thirty minutes, and there could be a long wait for offenders if drivers started signalling each other down the line.

The careless driver would be certain to show high speed on the counter because of the short distance between the hoses. At eighty-eight feet per second (sixty miles per hour) there is less than three-tenths of a second to react and slow the vehicle — simply impossible. Even a distance of fifty yards after recognition may not allow enough time to brake. The ease of using other speed metering systems has led to officer pressure for devices which are actually much easier for drivers to circumvent than the old hoses.

Orbis

On the opposite end of the officer difficulty scale is the infamous Orbis. The name is not an acronym, but comes from the Greek meaning "eye," and rightly so. Designed in about 1970 by Ling-Temco-Vought, the system consists of rows of contact switches placed in grooves cut across the roadway. These rows are 6 feet apart, and lie 110 feet in front of a 6 foot stanchion standing in the median strip. Inside a box atop the stanchion is a motor-driven 35mm camera, fitted with a 250mm lens. Orbis film is infrared-sensitive, and the camera is equipped with a strobe light having an IR-filtered 200 watt-second strobe. A polarizing filter on the lens is designed to cut glare from the approaching car's windshield, rendering the driver's face, if not more photogenic, at least more visible.

Should a car cross the contact switches at a speed over the set limit, the camera is tripped thirty-five milliseconds later. Under ideal conditions, the result is a clear, black and white picture of the car, plate, and driver. Date, time, speed limit, location and actual car speed are burned into the photo print electronically.

The first Orbis gauntlet was a ten mile stretch of Highway 303 near Arlington, Texas. The experiment began in mid-1970, and, after several court tests, was held to be admissible as prima facie evidence of a violation.

The original Texas layout used four installations, each able to cover one of the two lanes in each direction at one time. To prevent taking the same speeder's picture two to four times over the layout, only one undisclosed unit was in operation at any time. The units were placed two miles apart, the usual distance. The original installation was said to be more economical than patrolling. In 1971, the National Highway Traffic Safety Administration projected the annual cost of using the Orbis network to watch over the nation's one million most traveled highways as $300 million, or under one dollar per day per mile.

Big Brother would have planted plenty more of these ticket trees along the highways by now, except that Orbis turned out to have many drawbacks, not even counting the ethical ones. Costs for Orbis skyrocketed as all others did between 1970 and 1975, so a few relatively inexpensive tricks were conceived. Orbis-like installations were built, using dummy camera/computer boxes. Locations burned into the real photos were coded, to avoid revealing which were the working Orbis units. This program detracted from Orbis' evidential value in court. Currently, a stretch similar to the original would reportedly cost $27,000 to set up and over $270 per month to maintain, and more if all boxes were functioning. It would take an awful lot of speeding tickets to make it a going proposition.

It does not take local drivers very long to compare notes and tickets and figure out which traps are loaded and which are phony. Although the system was originally thought to be functional after dark, the angles of certain windshields defeated the small strobe. Larger light sources, even with IR filtration, were held to be a possible safety hazard. Few Orbis systems are consequently in use at night. Also, after dark, the natives sometimes become restless, and do strange and terrible things to poor Orbis, leaving him crippled, and adding considerably to the cost of his operation.

We probably have not heard the last of the Orbis concept. Robot-like enforcement seems to hold great allure for bureaucrats, who desire order above all else. Automotive design students who compete in government sponsored "Safety Car" competitions have been specifically asked for windshield-angle parameters that would improve visibility inward as well as outward. Somewhere in the future may lie a completely compatible car-road monitoring traffic system, courtesy of our wise congress. But, for now, Orbises are isolated curiosa along about twenty stretches of roads located in Texas, Massachusetts and New Jersey.

VASCAR

Still in use, but rapidly being replaced by radar, is the famous VASCAR. The name stands for: Visual Average Speed Computer And Recorder. The machine has one function: clocking the speed of one vehicle over a known distance, then computing and displaying the average speed to the officer-operator. It simply measures average speed over a known distance.

Most stopwatch chronographs feature a dial that reads speed directly in miles per hour when a button is pressed at the onset and finish of a mile. When fine tuning my car for racing, I used to take it over a measured mile while a friend operated the stopwatch. That was essentially a simplified VASCAR system.

Because the police want to clock over a much shorter distance, they select any two points to drive between, while their odometer feeds the distance into a combined electronic stopwatch and calculator. This technique allows the patrol car to be one of the distance reference points. It is common to find VASCAR equipped highway patrol cars posted above the highway on an overpass, or just about a quarter mile past one at the side of the road itself. Incidentally, the equipment is designed so that one quarter mile is the minimum distance that can be used. For example, a car approaches at 70 miles per hour on the overpass. The officer hits the time entry button. A moment later the car passes by the parked patrol car at 55 miles per hour, and the time entry is stopped. The vehicle's average speed of 62.50 comes up instantly in digital light display. Then Smokey can decide whether to give chase, radio ahead to another car or stay on station.

VASCAR has achieved such a mysterious reputation over the last decade because a skillful operator can use it in many different modes of patrol. Its uses can be varied to permit making either time or distance entries first, while both parties are moving. Time and distance entries can even be made while you and Smokey are driving in opposite directions.

Smokey can be ahead of you and note your car looming up in his mirror too quickly to suit him. So, he notes a roadside reference point and enters the next quarter mile or more of distance into the VASCAR computer mounted on his dash or console. He mentally notes the area of the road at the end of the quarter mile or more. As you pass the first point a few seconds later, he starts the time key. Perhaps ten seconds later, if you are doing over seventy miles per hour, he has stopped the key as you pass point B. By then you may see him and slow down, but he is already looking at the digital readout that shows seventy miles per hour in bright green numerals. Under ideal conditions, he can do this as you pass each other in opposite directions, but this is difficult and harder to sustain in court. Again, under ideal situations, these functions may even be performed at night. Many such convictions have stood.

The most common VASCAR moving technique, or mode, is following. The officer times the motorist as he passes any two reference points, and then keys in the distance as fed from his calibrated odometer while the officer goes through the same two points. This is the moving method which has been hardest to beat in court, because the officer can add testimony regarding speeds he may have had to travel to apprehend the suspect down the road, thereby adding pacing to the clocking.

Equally hard to beat are convictions obtained by stationary VASCAR posts, above or along the highway at night. After timing an automobile's approaching or receding lights through known distances, Smokey simply eases down the entrance ramp or into traffic behind the car.

If VASCAR is effective, and cannot be detected at a distance as radar can, then why is it being phased out? As with all other forms of visual clocking, the officer operating VASCAR has to be able to see a vehicle clearly in relation to the points. Distance, darkness, smog, or rain may interfere. Some of the techniques we have discussed require absolutely superb qualities of depth perception to pinpoint the crossing of reference points. This may be difficult for the officer to attest to in court. There are also a number of practical drawbacks, some of which were unheard of when VASCAR was designed and put into service. Primarily, VASCAR is becoming more and more inconvenient to use in the moving or patrol modes. Lowered highway speeds have actually contributed to clumping congestion, making clear observation of reference points more difficult. If the judge doubts that an officer was able to see both points, as well as the suspect vehicle, at all times, then he may dismiss the case. Since radar has become more prevalent, VASCAR is used more and more as a stationary ambush, and is therefore easier to spot and thwart by slowing down short of the second reference point to lower observed average speed. The problem, of course, is figuring out where that second reference point is. Not infrequently it is the police car itself, and if the cop can see you clearly, you can usually see him.

In summary, the accuracy, reliability, and general usefulness of VASCAR has often been criticized, espccially by the police themselves. Consequently, VASCAR is being rapidly replaced by that surest of all revenue producers, true moving radar.

Chapter IV
RADAR

Radar has become the most commonly used method of speed detection on our highway systems. We will devote this chapter to a consideration of its strengths, weaknesses and fallacies, followed by a section on countermeasures. A current educated guess is that there are more than 30,000 radar units presently in use in the United States.

How Radar Works

The term "radar" was coined from the initial letters of the phrase "radio detection and ranging." Short, very intense bursts or pulses of energy (radio waves) are sent out from a powerful radio transmitter. When these waves strike an object, a tiny fraction of the energy is reflected back to a radar receiver built in conjunction with the transmitter. The receiver is active between pulses. If an error in range of only five yards can be tolerated, time intervals must be measured with an accuracy of one thirtieth of one millionth of a second. Moving target radar relies on a fundamental principle of physics called the Doppler effect: when a radio wave of a particular frequency strikes a moving object, the result is an increase or a decrease of the frequency directly proportional to the speed of the object. This change in magnitude is referred to as the Doppler shift. As an object approaches, frequencies increase; as it recedes, they decrease. In either case, the shift is constant at 31.4 cycles per second per mile per hour. The radar set's computer counts the shift cycles for one second and divides by the Doppler constant of 31.4. It compares this to a preset speed, signals the officer by a buzzer, and locks in the speed reading on the computer face.

When a radar set is turned on, its beam first reflects back from the terrain and roadway. Whether the radar is moving or stationary, this initial reading is called the low Doppler, and forms the basis for comparison with approaching or receding objects. High Doppler simply refers to the amount of shift, either up or down, in received frequency. If a unit is the so-called moving radar, its computer will subtract low Doppler (the patrol car's own speed) from high Doppler shift and display the target's speed. If a car is approaching or receding at 100 miles per hour, its high Doppler is a shift of 3,140 cycles per second.

If some of this technical material escapes you, do not be concerned. It is neither essential for you or the police to understand the physics to operate or subvert the system.

Limitations of Radar

In the early sixties, one of the nation's largest aircraft companies wanted to check the speed of certain of their aircraft at the precise moment of takeoff. They contacted the local State Patrol Radar Division to help them obtain this information by using the radar equipment used for traffic control. It was found that the radar units were far too inaccurate to be helpful, although the state patrol certainly considered their units accurate enough to nail motorists.

But, alas — it is a different story today. Modern speed control radar units, if properly tuned, can provide double-checked readings in one fifth of a second, with better than ninety-nine percent accuracy, or one half of one mile per hour at 100 miles per hour, at ranges up to 3,000 feet, depending on the size of the target vehicle and the flatness of the terrain.

But, also alas — you have to cope with the officer's understanding of radar. Many years ago, I was ticketed by a moving patrol car equipped with stationary radar, as he approached me while traveling in the opposite direction. When I explained, and complained that his set was designed for him to use while stationary, he assured me that he often used the set in that manner. I knew the reading was incorrect, because I was actually going ten to fifteen miles per hour faster than he stated. Present electronic equipment is capable of those adjustments, but not back in those years.

A radar beam travels with the speed of light (about 186,000 miles per second) in a straight line. This means that police can not shoot radar beams around corners or over hills to track you; detection must be line of sight. Microwaves lose power in a geometrical ratio to distance, as does all radiated energy. Because of this, the maximum effective range of the modern police units is about 1,300 feet to discern an individual compact car, 2,000 feet for standard cars and 3,000 feet for full-size trucks in the clear.

Also, radar cannot work at ninety degrees. Targets must come within six degrees of beam center. Radar must concentrate on approaching and receding vehicles. Radar can penetrate light cover, like leaves, bushes, and of course glass. Cover does, however, decrease its effectiveness; for example, the use of radar inside the auto, operating through the window, is nearly a third less effective. Hills, large buildings and other massive obstructions will block radar. An officer operating a radar unit has a difficult time singling out a speeding car which is traveling into a group of slower moving autos, because the unit tends to focus on the entire group of cars as one target. The most attractive target to the radar is usually the biggest or the closest, rather than the fastest car within its range. Some vehicles are marginally more reflective than others. We say that they offer a greater radar cross-section, or that they have a denser outer surface. For instance, if a Ford Econoline Van and a Chevrolet Corvette are both traveling at seventy-five miles per hour, the 'vette will come several hundred feet closer to the radar before registering. Or, the van will register first, protecting the low profile fiberglass bodied car, if the two crest a hill abreast and enter a radar beam together. This is true even though both cars may have similar weights and lengths.

Even the group of cars itself can provide distorted readings. Reflections from vehicles traveling at slightly different speeds can cause the speed of an oncoming target to register at a higher speed than it is actually moving.

There are a number of things, both inside and outside the police vehicle, that can have a profound effect on radar readings. Unless the officer is aware of these, you could get stung with a bad rap.

An air conditioner in operation in the police cruiser can produce inaccurate readings, as can vibrations from the transmission under certain circumstances. A heater fan motor can create an electrical field that can trigger some radar units, causing them to register a reading of thirty-five miles per hour with no traffic in sight. Audio frequencies can also change the radar scope readout. For example, by whistling into the radar antenna or the microphone of a police CB radio, various readings can be produced on the digital panel; speeds up to eighty-eight miles per hour have been recorded.

High tension power lines in the vicinity of the clocking can raise havoc, as can flashing roadside advertising signs. Also, thunderstorms, short wave radio bounce, and other natural phenomena can all affect the accuracy of radar.

For over twenty years the courts have accepted radar evidence without question. It is interesting to note that the U.S. Department of Transportation is currently undertaking a study of the accuracy and validity of police radar through the National Bureau of Standard's Law Enforcement Standards Laboratory in Rockville, Maryland. They expect to release their results sometime in 1979. Seems a bit late for a lot of people, does it not?

The efficiency and range of radar depends largely on the wavelength used. All present traffic radar units emit microwaves in one of three frequencies — S-, X-, or K-Band. As the equipment has become more sophisticated, the wave frequency has been increased to provide greater penetration and less dispersion. The original units emitted a radio wave of low frequency (2 Billion, 455 million cycles per second or 2.455 Gigahertz or GHz) called the S-Band. Most operating highway units today (about ninety-seven percent) employ the X-Band (10.525 GHz). This is also sometimes referred to as the new Military Standard #463 "J" Band frequency. The newest instruments, primarily the hand held sets, use the K-Band (24.150 GHz), which may well be the radar microwave frequency of the future.

The Units Themselves

Traffic radar appeared in the early 1950's. For many years, these speed meters were only licensed to be operated at 2.455 GHz. These S-Band instruments stood on a tripod near the shoulder of the road and had a power output of approximately 200 mw. They could only clock accurately at distances of about 175 feet. Early traffic radars made by Decatur, Motorola and others were fragile radio tube types, using ink-stylus paper graphs. Cars had to be specially modified to use these sets, and then were often out of service while the radar was being repaired. Sets were often disabled by normal patrol driving so radar cars were generally considered lost to regular patrol duties.

Early radar units were hard to set up, easy for motorists to spot, and had the attendant effect of keeping a patrol car off its beat. In those days, the cost of a police radar unit was about twice the cost of a 1955 Ford Police Interceptor, or about $3,000. Officers using these old stationary radars had to be relatively knowledgeable about electronics simply to operate them. The early units tipped the scales at about 250 pounds.

In about 1961, a new speed meter mounted inside or on the patrol car side window began to make its appearance, in very limited production. Prices went down fast during the transistorized sixties, and reliability went up. By 1965, a number of fairly compact, easily mounted meter sets, made by firms like Decatur and TECO, were being used on stationary mode in most states. These units were broadcasting the more effective X-Band signals, a frequency now authorized for speed detection equipment. These sets feature improved circuitry, considerably more power, and much greater range. With a power output of approximately fifty mw, these instruments had speed detection capabilities of short range (150 feet), medium range (300 feet), and long range (500-600 feet).

In 1970, traffic radar came of age. Prior to this, all police radar units used a chart or needle to show speed. Kustom Signals, Inc. of Chanute, Kansas introduced the TR-6 stationary unit. It had a sophisticated computer that figured and froze on-screen speed readings. It was, and is, extremely simple to use and transfer from car to car, at only five pounds per antenna and five pounds per readout unit. It is advertised to be accurate to one tenth of a mile per hour. This is the nation's most widely used police radar unit.

In 1972, Kustom produced a more advanced machine, known as the MR-7 Mobile Radar. This is the so-called "moving radar" or "new VASCAR," and sells presently for $2,385.00. It has all the features of VASCAR on moving patrol with much greater ease of operation, and can be used for stationary radar just as well as the older units. Its transmitter/receiver/antenna is mounted out the left rear window, and its dash-mounted, digital readout computer can check an oncoming car's speed in one fifth of a second. It even buzzes to tell the officer when a target within its 2,500 foot range is exceeding a preset limit keyed into the radar. It too operates in the X-Band.

In 1975, in a burst of enthusiasm, Kustom introduced the HR-8 hand held unit for $1,358.00. Mainly used at close ranges within municipalities, this gun radar uses the ultra high K-Band frequency. Although it is a very portable 4.3 pounds, it cannot be used in actual mobile patrol. However, it usually is operated at such close ranges that a motorcycle or chase car officer can take the speed reading, place the gun unit on the seat or into a saddlebag, and apprehend the speeder in a matter of seconds.

The Decatur Electronics RA-GUN is a compact, hand held (or car mounted), gun-shaped radar unit, which boasts direct digital readout in a small window located where the hammer mechanism appears on a conventional gun. The officer calibrates the unit with a tuning fork, flips on the battery pack, and points the unit at a moving object. Zappo — you are clocked within a 3,000 foot range.

Kustom Signals accounts for approximately fifty percent of all U.S. radar sales. Their latest offering is the MR-9 moving radar, not yet widely distributed. Other units, like the Smith & Wesson Digidar I and the Stoelting Speed Timer EVA IV, are also in use today for clocking speeders.

Incidentally, do not worry about the double-tubed, fore and aft radarscope you sometimes hear about. It simply does not exist.

The Essential Calibration

With all current X-band and K-Band units, the officer operating the radar must calibrate it at the beginning of his shift. A tuning fork supplied by the manufacturer is used. Each serial-numbered fork will vibrate at a known speed signal. For example, Kustom Signals supplies certified forks that are rated at 35, 50, 65 or 100 miles per hour frequencies (actually artificial high Doppler signals). The radar set is turned on and the fork is struck, then held a few inches in front of the antenna. The reading must be exact, or the unit is not put into service for that day.

Once a stationary location is set up, a second internal calibration is checked. This is a signal generated by a built-in crystal that also registers a speed on the readout unit's digital display. For instance, the Kustom MR-7 moving radar internal calibration can be checked at any time while on patrol. The usual interval for checking is about every ten speed readings. A complete calibration check should not take more than about a minute.

In both stationary and moving radar operation, the next step is to set the speed select. On the highway, a very zealous officer could set it for fifty-five miles per hour, but most do not. Depending on the particular state or locale and its policies, which change from time to time, grace allowances may vary from two to ten miles per hour over the limit. There are still many sympathetic officers who prefer to apprehend flagrant or erratic drivers, rather than give moderate speeders undue consideration. But, federal pressure and the ease of radar revenue collection have a way of eroding gentlemanly outlook.

The Range

Figures given for the range of traffic radar are often conflicting and confusing, varying from a few hundred to 5,000 feet. While it is true that the radar microwaves will extend as far as 5,000 feet under ideal conditions, at that distance they are too weak and diffused to be of any practical value in speed detection. The estimates of a few hundred feet belong either to the early radar units, or setups just over a hill or around a curve where range is limited on purpose.

There are two important considerations to keep in mind when contemplating practical radar range. One is that the radar signal emanates from a point source and spreads like a fan or funnel to cover increasingly wider areas. At 100 feet, the beam width extends across a two-lane highway. By the time 1,500 feet are reached, the beam width has spread to cover a four-lane highway, and dispersion considerably weakens the signal much beyond this. The maximum normal operational range for the best radar units is at about 1,500 feet, and most of the passenger car speeds are recorded, and arrests made, on the basis of distances of 1,000 feet or less. If the target is large enough, however, like a big semi, a tracking distance of 2,000 to 2,500 feet is possible, if the conditions are right.

The second point to remember is that, since radar locks in on the strongest signal, which is not necessarily the fastest car in a group, a visual confirmation by the officer is necessary. This has been supported and confirmed by the courts. The alleged offender must consequently be within the visual range of the officer, which limits the radar range to something less than 1,700 feet. Of interest in this regard is that observation ranges of a quarter mile (1,320 feet) are generally used in police radar setup courses, such as Kustom's "prefect" pre-use seminar. At 1,000 feet, offenders are fairly easy to identify, and the signal is strong enough to give accurate readings.

In the courtroom, a highway patrol officer can honestly testify that his X-Band beam was 110 feet wide at 1,000 feet, or almost large enough in diameter to cover four lanes. The K-Band beam is narrower. Designed for selectivity in congested traffic in municipal surroundings, the hand held radar gun is not commonly used for highway monitoring. At 1,000 feet (about one fifth mile), the beam of K-Band radar covers about two lanes of roadway.

The Stationary Mode

Most of the necessary aspects of stationary radar have already been covered, but a few comments on location are in order. A radar trap can be a solitary police car acting as both the detector and pursuit car, or can be a setup with a radar car and one or more pursuit cars farther down the road. Vehicles can be clocked in either an approaching or departing mode, but not ordinarily in both at the same time. While it is theoretically possible to swing a window mounted unit around quickly, in practice this is not done. Departing mode usage is not common, because the radar unit can so frequently be spotted before the clocking is accomplished.

The police will naturally attempt to pick highway surrounding that conceal their vehicles. By far the most common location is just over the crest of a small hill. Cops also like to hide around freeway curves; and beware of freeway ramps, particularly entrance ramps. Overpasses are danger areas too — sometimes the radar car is on top, sometimes hidden in the shadows underneath. Keep in mind that Smokey dislikes waiting in sun-scorched sedans, and expect traps to be set in shady surroundings when the weather is sunny and hot.

One of the trickier police strategies is to park a radar car across the dividing median strip, sometimes with a guard rail in-between. While its positioning lulls you into feeling secure and inaccessible, the pursuit cars are running down speeders a short distance down the pike, on your side of the freeway.

Radar traps are far more common in areas close to cities, generally within two or three miles. There are several reasons for this: cities and towns offer the patrolmen coffee stops, lunch, toilets and other conveniences; the occasional uncooperative driver can be taken to a nearby police station, and these areas have the greatest concentration of motorists. Areas with little traffic seldom have radar traps, simply because it would not be economical.

The Moving Mode

Moving radar has not become nearly as formidable a threat to the motorist as many originally anticipated it would. In the first place, sitting in a parked car is a lot easier than engaging in patrol work. Besides, radar is easier to use and interpret in a stationary mode. Moving radar is never pointed backward to clock rear-to-front; it will not work that way. Moving mode is always set up either outside the driver's window or above the passenger side seat, aimed at a slight angle into the oncoming traffic.

Two modes, pacing and approaching, can be employed while in motion. The pacing radar is of little value over conventional pacing, except that by matching speeds with the suspect vehicle and reading the radar dial, the patrolman can confirm the speed of the car he is clocking. The police radar car must not be traveling faster than the suspect, or the readings are meaningless. Pacing mode is consequently not popular with the police.

The approaching mode presents other problems. In order to secure reliable readings, the police unit must travel five, or, more likely, ten miles per hour more slowly than the selected speed for oncoming vehicles. For example, if the officer sets the select for sixty miles per hour, he must cruise at about fifty miles per hour. While this does encourage the police to stay within the speed limits — certainly a substantial blessing — it also ordinarily results in a pack of cars clustering behind or around him (which tends to be a dead giveaway, as well as slowing traffic flow). If you encounter a similar setup or spot radar protruding from a police car window when you are rounding a curve, or for some other reason are out of direct line with the radar's beam, decelerate as quickly as possible. Creative Marketing Corp. of Texas states that "Rapid deceleration will cause the unit to display a solid line instead of speed." Experts say that this deceleration must be at a rate of at least 3.15 miles per hour per second to be effective. While this requires brakes, it is not a particularly rapid deceleration, equivalent to braking from 70 to 55 miles per hour in 4.76 seconds.

Keep in mind that the radar beam must be directed at you for it to work. So — if the police car is going downhill, its beam is directed to the bottom of the hill or in the dip. If you are approaching it, speeding down the hill toward the dip, you are safe until the beam levels out at you. The same sort of thing occurs around curves. These situations give you time to slow down if you see a radar unit coming.

If, on the other hand, you are in direct line with him, the element of closing speed gives you less time to react, even if you detect his beam with a microwave detector.

Another problem with the approaching mode of moving radar is that if the officer does detect a speeder, he must make a U turn to give chase. Under many conditions this may be impractical because of traffic, and is usually impossible in divided lane freeways. So, as you can see, moving radar as presently constructed and used is less than ideal.

Radar Detectors

Once, driving along a road, I came upon a big, crude, hand-lettered sign tacked to a tree that read, "Watch Out. Radar Trap Ahead." And sure enough, there it was, a few blocks further down. Some irate citizen had decided to warn his fellow drivers. I wonder what the cops thought when all of a sudden everyone was law abiding. Since you cannot count on that kind of help very often, we had better look for other ways.

Microwaves travel in a straight line, so theoretically you can see the sending unit when it is shooting waves at you. I say theoretically, because often the unit is not very obvious. While it is important to look down the road for parked cars, most units are reasonably well hidden. An open trunk used to be significant, because a unit would often be mounted there, but that is no longer the case. Truck weigh stations and some highway overpasses often used to have stands for radar, but these systems are virtually obsolete. Some states are big on radar, some are not.

But — do not despair. If radar is a problem in your area or proposed area of travel, I would suggest a microwave detector. It was in the middle fifties that police began to commonly use radar. During the following five years several microwave detectors appeared, but were impractical, either because of size, weight, unreliability, or for other reasons. However, there are currently several companies catering to this demand with a variety of sophisticated electronic devices.

In studying the detection range claims made by various manufacturers, you will notice considerable, sometimes confusing, variation. Accurate figures are indeed difficult to predict, not only because of the screening effects of trees, hills, billboards, and other obstacles when the detectors are used in actual practice, but also because of the variation in the output power of different police radar units. And even when we know the radar power output, we find that most police units miss theoretical efficiency by twenty-five to thirty-five percent. Even so, most of the manufacturers advertise that their detection will be at least twice the distance at which you are likely to be tracked. Tracking distances are usually 1,000 to 1,500 feet for passenger cars, and up to about 2,500 feet for trucks.

In 1961, Radatron Corp. of New York began producing a practical model for about forty dollars called the Radar Sentry. It issues a warning beep (700 cycle tone) when it detects microwaves in either the 2.455 GHz or 10.550 GHz frequency. Battery operated, it clips onto the sun visor. Its range of about one quarter mile was adequate to allow sufficient warning against the old "S" (2.455 GHz) and "X" (10.525 GHz) police radar units, but the newer units with ranges up to 3,000 feet are another story. Studies have shown that if the police set up for 2,500 feet (about one half mile), the Radar Sentry gives a weak signal about a tenth of a mile before the police recording, and a loud warning beep one quarter mile after you have been clocked. Not too reassuring! However, as we pointed out earlier, conditions do not usually allow the police to set up for maximum range. More recently, Radatron has offered several updated pieces of equipment. In addition to their old Radar Sentry, they now have the Senturion, and feature the Radar Sentry XK at the top of their line.

Sometime around 1973, Autotronics, Inc. of Texas produced their Snooper, a long range radar detector of excellent quality, now worth about ninety dollars. This device operates off the car's twelve volt electrical system, either through direct connection or by way of a cigarette lighter plug. The Snooper has a calculated range of 3,520 feet, giving a signal beep at least 500 feet before the commonly used police radar units could track you. While this does not seem like a lot of warning if you are moving at an enthusiastic pace, let me point out that on dry pavement at seventy miles per hour, you can expect to travel about seventy-seven feet between your impulse to stop and the time your foot reaches the brake pedal. Assuming you have good brakes, another 381 feet will streak by before you come to a *complete stop.* You should consequently be able to easily brake down to the speed limit with a 500 foot warning.

In 1975, in response to the new K-Band frequencies used by some police departments, Autotronics introduced the Super Snooper. This is an exceptionally sensitive detector with a range substantially in excess of one mile. Be prepared to pay about $150 for this sophisticated item. Autotronics claims that their instruments will provide more than twice the warning time of any other radar detector on the market, while maintaining a ninety-nine percent rejection of signal sources other than radar.

The Eliminator models are manufactured by former employees of Autotronics, in a firm called Creative Marketing Corporation. Their Eliminator model (X-Band), at about $80 per copy, produces a warning beep, while their Super Eliminator (X- and K-Band), at about $150, features both beep and glow lamp, and claims a detection range of up to three miles.

Recently several new detector manufacturers have appeared on the scene: Whistler, Inc. of Littleton, Massachusetts; ComRadar Corp. of Dayton, Ohio; Controls Unlimited, Inc. of Arlington Heights, Illinois; and Radio Shack (A Tandy corporation).

Whistler produces the Whistler Radar Eye, operating on the X-Band, and ComRadar offers two Fox models. Their tiny Fox II picks up X-Band. Their Fox II Remote is designed for X- and K-Bands, and comes with a remote receiver-antenna, so that it can be mounted at some distance from the buzzer, warning light, and squelch control.

Controls Unlimited offers a model called The Long Ranger. Dash or visor mounted, it provides audio and visual warning for X-Band for $129.95.

Radio Shack sells a detector called Road Patrol for $69.95, which in appearance and features seems nearly identical to Autotronics' Snooper model.

Dale Smith, president of Electrolert, Inc. of Ohio, tells an interesting tale of how he got into the radar detection field. He had been instrumental in designing some of the first police radar units used for speed detection. Shortly thereafter, as Dale was cruising down a roadway, a speeding truck overtook him, but swung in behind when a police radar unit appeared up ahead. Dale, being the first vehicle in line, was given the speeding ticket, a victim of the strong signal generated by the truck, and of police misinterpretation. Thus began a vindictive career in radar detection devices. Electrolert claims that they do eighty percent of the detection business in the U.S. Presently they market two units, both operating from the vehicle's twelve volt system (direct connection or cigar lighter adapter connection), and both capable of detection in excess of one mile, depending on the radar output power. Their Fuzzbuster (selling for about a C note) features a visual, light warning system when radar is encountered transmitting in X-Band.

Probably the best detector on the market today is Electrolert's "Fuzzbuster II Multi-Band." Its creators foresaw the possibility of new police radar frequencies, and so incorporated in this instrument a solid-state scanner that can receive any police microwave frequency allowed by the FCC - the entire range between nine GHz and twenty-five GHz. The electronic battle is on!

What do you look for in a radar detector? I have included a chart which summarizes the features of the thirteen currently available detectors. You will notice that only the more expensive models will detect both K-Band and X-Band. At present, X-Band is still the radar frequency used for most highway traps, with the K-Band reserved for municipal hand held gun use. I do, however, expect that the future will see a greater use of K-Band. If you can afford the extra bucks, it could be a good investment. All worthwhile units connect to the car's twelve volt system, either directly or via the cigar lighter. Self-contained battery strength is unreliable.

Visual or audio alert? It depends on your preference and on where the unit is mounted. The best units feature both. If you have more than one vehicle, it is nice to be able to switch the unit around easily, and various units give you this option. A good electronic damping system to eliminate most of the nonradar noises is almost essential, if a large percentage of your driving is done in congested signal areas particularly enriched by CB radio. Some units do a better job of this than others.

Information Unlimited of Amherst, New Hampshire has developed a do-it-yourself kit. They will sell you the inner components of a "Police Radar Trap Detector #RT 8" and also "Kit RT 80K" for about thirty dollars, and furnish a casing very similar in design to that of a Snooper. Such units can be particularly valuable for concealed installations in those states and locales where radar detectors are prohibited.

Truckers often solve this problem by mounting the detector out of sight under the cab. This often permits pickup of radar signals from behind as well as ahead, as the scatter becomes trapped between the roadway and undercarriage. If your auto is too lowslung or may be used off-road, a kit offers a chance to mount a sensing antenna in a mock light well, with power supply and signal devices installed in unused accessory locations on your dash. Or you could use a ventilation grid just under the windshield, or a fake hood air scoop, opened to permit a cooling airflow past the device.

Kit adaptations may also be the answer for those drivers who feel the need for both a front and rear facing detector. Many truckers are using dual setups in areas with heavy radar. Another expedient is an accessory reflective tape applied to the windshield just above the forward facing waveguide, to catch the signal scatter from radar approaching from the rear, or across a switchback curve. Recent car magazine articles attest to heavy radar contact along all axes of main roads, every few miles in the deep south. Eastern seaboard states are often as bad. California does not permit their state highway patrols to use radar, but local communities use it.

All in all, in purchasing a radar detecting device, you pretty much get what you pay for, as long as you are dealing with a reputable manufacturer. It is not unreasonable to expect a warranty of six months to a year on any of the devices.

Police Dirty Tricks

Unfortunately, there are several methods the police can use to counteract the effectiveness of radar detectors. Because there are still relatively few vehicles equipped with detectors, however, the police usually do not go to great lengths to subvert them.

One method Smokey could employ would be to place the speed meter so that it records departing vehicles rather than approaching or oncoming cars. This requires a hidden radar unit. You could be stymied because your radar detector ordinarily only received in one direction, and even if you had reflective tape or a rearward detector, you could be clocked and warned simultaneously.

Another method is for the traffic officer to point the speed meter into the highway at a forty to forty-five degree angle. While this technique greatly reduces the range and maximum speed readings of the meter, it also greatly reduces your ability to detect his radar.

As we have previously mentioned, since radar only travels in a straight line, the police often try to subvert both the observant motorist who is looking far down the road for a parked car and the microwave detector, by placing their radar unit just around a curve or over a hill. Their rationale is that by the time you have spotted or detected them, they have already clocked you. This, unfortunately, does catch the observant motorist, but usually not the guy with the microwave detector. The reason is that the cops have greatly reduced their range with this positioning, and there are enough high energy microwaves bounced and scattered around the hilltop or curve to trigger off even relatively insensitive detectors in time for a slowdown.

The hand held gun unit, directed at a single car only, emits a single burst of microwave energy, and you are almost instantly clocked, negating the value of a detector; but these devices are used primarily in cities where the savvy driver should not be speeding anyway.

Although I do not believe it is being done, the radar speed meter manufacturers could shift wave polarization in future models, feeding cross-polarized waves to a microwave detector, thereby reducing its sensitivity by ten to twelve db.

An evolving problem is the new generation of police radar units that are tuned slightly outside the X- and K-Band frequencies allowed by the FCC. They are not far enough astray to upset the government, but they could prevent finely tuned detectors from picking up a signal. However, the all-band, scanning detector, already mentioned, would pick up the signal.

Another problem is the soon to be introduced car-mounted radar models that send out only an intermittent beam, like the hand held HR-8. These are virtually undetectable by radar detectors until it is too late.

A homemade application of the intermittent beam principle is now in operation by some ingenious police officers. What they do is point their stationary, continuous beam radar unit down the road, turn it on, and then cover the sending antenna with a microwave oven cooking pan. When they see a car coming, they remove the pan for an instant to clock their adversary. Consequently, the approaching driver with a microwave detector would get a warning only at the instant of his "capture."

A final dirty trick employed by the police is the use of decoy microwave transmitters. These devices keep your radar detector and you in a semi-constant state of irritability, never knowing what is real and what is phony in the radar clocking department. They come in various forms. Tennessee has rigged twenty-five to thirty unmanned, outdated, but still serviceable radar units along certain highways. Iowa presently uses inexpensive, twenty-five dollar units, at various strategic locations along their roads. Washington State has gone an expensive, sophisticated step further in the decoy business. Police there are presently employing solar battery powered microwave transmitters, contained in plastic boxes about eighteen inches square. These devices go for $300 each and they expect to deploy over 200 of them around the state by hanging them from trees and fences near the highways. However, I have a hunch they may become sought after collector's items, a source for electrical components, or victims of a well-aimed vandal's pellet.

There are also less hostile methods to cope with these devices. The most obvious is to simply slow down for the several thousand feet beamed by the decoy as you would for a radar unit, and then resume cruising speed — no great hardship.

If these devices become excessively prevalent, I would expect the more progressive radar detector manufacturers to produce an instrument capable of detecting the difference, perhaps one with a more narrow pattern of reception, so that it would be triggered only by beams coming from a few feet off the roadway, the height of police radar.

The Fallacies

Quite a number of myths have developed over the years concerning detection by radar. While I can not hope to include them all, as they develop on almost a day to day basis, I will try to mention and dispel the most common of these.

I recently encountered the most ridiculous story I have heard so far when a young friend asked me quite seriously if radar could be foiled by smearing the front bumper with peanut butter. Perhaps he thought the police digital panel would light up with the green letters, CHUNKY.

According to one theory, radar is used to detect a shell of electrons traveling with your car, so if you use a ground chain or conductive strip you will escape detection. A nice bit of pseudoscience, but without basis in fact.

A well-known, but useless, practice involves using aluminum foil to wrap the car aerial or stuff hubcaps in order to escape radar detection. The idea for this probably came from the use of aluminum foil strips (called chaff) dumped from aircraft in World War II, designed to confuse radar. This worked, but only by clouding or shadowing the enemy radar screen. It would work for you, too, if you dumped a barrel of aluminum strips from your car at the appropriate moment. Instead of a speeding charge you would get life for littering.

There is also a theory that radar will not detect a fiberglass car, because it only works on metal. This, of course, is not true. Radar detects even heavy cloud formations. Fiberglass is marginally less dense than metal, and tends to give a slightly weaker signal, but only slightly. Certain materials, do, however, either absorb or cancel microwaves, and were used by the Germans to camouflage U-Boats during World War II. Unfortunately these materials do not seem to be available for civilian automobiles.

Some believe that an automobile equipped with a radio transmitter cannot be detected by radar. This is not true unless the radio is equipped for electronic jamming by transmitting suitably timed signals on the appropriate frequency. While the creation of a police radar jamming device is easily within the capability of electronic technology, expense and questions of legality may be insurmountable problems. What I am really waiting for is an instrument that would detect the police microwaves and then return a streak of high energy particles, like a laser beam, that would melt his radar unit, and perhaps his badge.

Jamming

While I cannot truly recommend the electronic jamming of police radar units, it is an intriguing idea. There are several electronic enthusiasts who have improvised radar signal generators from microwave oven tubes and power assemblies. When such a device is mounted in a dish reflector, and the signal projected through openings in a car's grill toward a police receiver, the effect on Smokey's computer is truly electrifying. So much more Doppler returns than was sent that the speed readout commonly reacts by totaling up some large multiple of the true speed - say, 777 for 70 miles per hour.

Although no court in the land would be likely to convict you for doing 777 miles per hour in your Olds 98, think what the fine would be if they did! The real problem, of course, is that you might be convicted of the federal crime of unlicensed radio transmission, and possibly for other FCC violations, nicking you with a $10,000 fine.

Unfortunately, the police are already sufficiently aware of this multiple readout effect to make its use safe only in a very congested area, where many cars would fall under suspicion of having a jamming device. Your speed would probably be low under those driving conditions, anyway. If you zap The Man's radar on a fine, fast, solitary run through upper Arizona, he is going to want to stop you just to find out how you did it. What these devices really do is make your car unmistakable under observation, and convert a minor sort of traffic case into a federal offense. Do not try it.

In theory, there is another, more sophisticated, jamming method. Although the technology for its exists, nothing employing the method is presently available. The principle goes like this: as we have previously mentioned, police X-Band operates at 10.525 GHz, and detects speeders by a frequency shift in the reflected beam. There is a shift of 31.4 Hz for each one mile per hour, or a shift of 1,727 Hz for fifty-five miles per hour. Consequently, if you had a superbly accurate transmitter issuing a frequency of 10.525 GHz plus 0.000001727 GHz, or 10.525001727 GHz, the digital readout on the police radar scope would list your speed as fifty-five miles per hour, regardless of how fast you were going.

To be really useful, such a transceiver should have the capability of manufacturing different frequencies, so that you could announce any number of speeds to the police, depending on speed limits and circumstances.

I am afraid, however, the FCC would frown mightily on such a device, as would several other government agencies.

Radar Legalese

As you may have noticed, this book includes a chapter on legal aspects, written by an attorney; but since there are so many laws, precedents, and incidents specifically related to radar, I have included this section to answer some of the general questions commonly asked.

Traffic radar of some kind is currently employed in all fifty states, and all but ten (Alaska, Arkansas, Hawaii, Indiana, Massachusetts, Nevada, New Jersey, New Mexico, Utah, and West Virginia) also employ moving radar. Probably by the time you read this many of those named will have expanded their usage.

The legal use of radar for traffic control has been challenged in all the states, and many landmark cases have been judged. New Jersey versus Dantonio established radar admissibility. The Commonwealth of Kentucky versus Honeycutt case established all the essential functional points: "a properly constructed and operated radar device is capable of measuring accurately the speed of a motor vehicle; the tuning fork test is an accurate method of determining accuracy; it is sufficient to qualify an operator that he have such knowledge and training as enables him properly to set up, test and read the instrument; it is not required that the operator understand the scientific principles of radar or be able to explain its internal workings, and that a few hours instruction normally should be enough to qualify an operator; and the officer's estimate of excessive speed, from visual observation, when confirmed by the reading of the radar device and when the offending vehicle is out front, by itself, nearest the unit, is sufficient to identify the vehicle if the officer's observations support the radar evidence."

This decision in effect allowed the government to equip police with sophisticated devices which they did not have to understand permitting possible abuse by well-meaning officers. It became much harder, although not impossible, to cast doubt on a radar operator's testimony after this judgment. In order to legally fault radar being employed by a qualified operator, you must convince the judge or jury that either the unit was malfunctioning, or that the officer failed to visually establish that the offending vehicle was out in front, by itself, nearest the unit.

Recently, in Washington State, a radar electronics technician challenged the accuracy of individual police radar units. In court he referred to the two standard radar calibration tests: (1) the calibration button on the unit itself, and (2) the tuning fork test. He pointed out that the first depends entirely on the unproven accuracy of the radar set crystal oscillator, which must be checked in a laboratory with certified equipment to prove accuracy. He explained that the second test depended on the accuracy of a tuning fork carried in a shaking, vibrating, jostling patrol car, capable of throwing it out of frequency. He contested his ticket and won the case. Since then, eight out of eleven cases using the same argument have won, so maybe there is hope after all.

There is a radar trap situation that occasionally comes up which you should keep in mind, involving two police cars: a radar car clocking automobiles, and a pursuit car driven by a ticketing officer. A friend of mine tells the story succinctly. He had been clocked by a hidden radar unit and then picked up by the intercept patrol car officer a short distance away, who charged him and issued the ticket. When he appeared in court and the judge asked for his plea, he stated, "Not guilty." He pleaded his own case in a few words. He asked the arresting officer how he had known he was speeding.

"The officer with the radar unit radioed to me," came the answer.

"In other words, you gave me a ticket on the basis of hearsay evidence. Isn't that correct?"

Before the officer could answer, the judge said, "Case dismissed."

At the other end of the spectrum is the question of the legality of radar or microwave detectors. Because these instruments do not transmit radio signals, no operator licensing is required. However, in spite of this, even the simple possession has been declared illegal in Connecticut, Virginia, Denver Colorado, and Washington D.C. Some 4,000 radar detectors have been seized without recompense under the Virginia law. These laws are still awaiting a constitutional challenge. The outcome is indefinite.

Electrolert, Inc. is conducting a well financed war against all

44

such anti-radar detector laws. If you are harrassed by police for the possession or use of a detector, Electrolert will supply you with advice and material to handle the case yourself, or, in certain landmark cases, even furnish a lawyer.

New Jersey took a devious approach to outlawing radar detectors, passing a windshield obstruction law to prohibit the mounting of any device on a vehicle's dash or windshield. Naturally, there are ways to mount detectors to subvert this law.

There are a couple of federal laws that might be applied to the use of radar detectors that could further complicate things. One is the law that prohibits you from telling others what you have heard on a radio or from using any information that you might have heard for your personal gain. This could conceivably apply to microwave detection, your personal gain being the avoidance of a ticket. Also, this law could make the CB transmission about radar traps illegal, if so interpreted.

Another is the federal law against using a police monitor or any other receiver (radar detector?) to help you commit a crime. This offense is punishable by ten to twenty years in a Federal Prison or a fine of $10,000, or both.

As far as I know, neither of these laws has been exercised in this regard. Thank goodness! However, despite screams of "foul" by the enforcement authorities, 500,000 detectors have been sold so far, and expectations are that over one million will be in use by the end of the year.

	SENTURION	SNOOPER	FUZZBUSTER	ELIMINATOR	RADAR SENTRY	FOX 11
WAVE DETECTED	X	X	X	X	X	X
MANUFACTURER	RADATRON CORP. 2424 Niagara Falls Blvd. North Tonawanda, N.Y. 14120	AUTOTRONICS, INC. 1399 Executive Drive West Richardson, Texas 75031	ELECTROLERT, INC. 4949 South 25A Troy, Ohio 45373	CREATIVE MARKETING CORP. 2880 LBJ, Suite 307 Dallas, Texas 75234	RADATRON CORP.	COMRADAR CORP. 4518 Taylorsville Rd. Dayton, Ohio 45424
SELF-CONTAINED BATTERY	No	No	No	No	Yes	No
POWERED BY 12 Volt ELECTR. SYSTEM	Yes	Yes	Yes	Yes	No	Yes
POWER INDICATOR LIGHT	No	No	Yes	No	No	No
AUDIO ALERT	Yes	Yes	No	Yes	Yes	Yes
VISUAL ALERT	Yes	Yes	Yes	No	No	Yes
SENSITIVITY (SQUELCH) CONTROL	Yes	Yes	Yes	Yes	Yes	Yes
PRICE	$109.95	$89.95	$109.95	$79.95	$40.00	$129.00
MOUNTING	Sunvisor clip or dash	Windshield, dash or windshield molding	Windshield or dash	Windshield or dash	Sunvisor clip	Sunvisor clip
CAR TO CAR TRANSFER CAPABILITY	Yes (sunvisor mount only)	Yes	Yes	Yes	Yes	Yes

	RADAR SENTRY XK	SUPER SNOOPER	SUPER ELIMINATOR	FOX 11 REMOTE	WHISTLER RADAR EYE MODEL RE-55	WHISTLER RADAR EYE MODEL RE-55 XK	FUZZBUSTER 11 MULTI-BAND
WAVE DETECTED	X and K	X and K	X and K	X and K	X	X and K	All Bands
MANUFACTURER	RADATRON CORP.	AUTOTRONICS, INC.	CREATIVE MARKETING CORP.	COMRADAR CORP.	WHISTLER, INC. P.O. Box 37 Littleton, Mass. 01460	WHISTLER, INC. P.O. Box 37 Littleton, Mass. 01460	ELECTROLERT, INC.
SELF-CONTAINED BATTERY	No	No	No	No	No	No	No
POWERED BY AUTO 12 Volt ELECTR. SYSTEM	Yes	Yes	Yes	Yes	Yes	Yes	Yes
POWER INDICATOR LIGHT	Yes	Yes	Yes	No	System test button instead	System test button instead	No
AUDIO ALERT	Yes	Yes	Yes	Yes	Yes	Yes	Yes
VISUAL ALERT	Yes	Yes	Yes	Yes	Yes	Yes	Yes
SENSITIVITY (SQUELCH) CONTROL	Yes	Yes	Yes	Yes	No	No	Yes
PRICE	$149.95	$149.95	149.95	$169.95	$99.95	$159.95	$129.95
MOUNTING	Sunvisor or dash	Windshield or dash	Windshield or dash	Various locations	Sunvisor or dash	Sunvisor or dash	Dash mount
CAR TO CAR TRANSFER CAPABILITY	Yes (sunvisor mount only)	Yes	Yes	Yes	No	Yes	Yes

Chapter V
Citizen Band Radio

This discussion is a condensed survey of mobile radio communications and hints on selection and installation of such gear. It would take a huge volume to do more than introduce the reader to the basics of CB radio. The intention of this chapter is to stress the use of CB and/or single side band as an adjunct in traversing roads rapidly and safely without legal entanglements.

The Extent of It All

There are now about twenty-nine million CB transmitters licensed in the U.S. Perhaps five million operate in Canada, and some of the states in Mexico now allow ownership of CB's. In America, about one in twenty trucks uses AM/CB, or its cousin, single side band. Together, these users constitute a gigantic road intelligence network, with the truckers providing the most consistent regular reports on bear migrations.

From our standpoint, monitoring the net with a simple converter may be more important than the ability to join in the ratchet-jawing. It is especially important when in the deep south or in the eastern corridor, where speed traps are particularly common. In states like California, where highway patrols use relatively little VASCAR and no radar, Smokey reports are the main way of knowing whether you are coming up on a patrol car which is stopped and busy, or one which is sweeping through your sector looking for violators.

All over the U.S. road net, CB channel 19, and often 21, are frequented by truckers coming on the air with road reports, and leaving to converse with one another on other frequencies. They are pretty good about discipline on channel 19, and it is a best bet for current road information as you monitor. If you are in convoy with other drivers or curious about other vehicles which seem to be in communication, channel 11, the national calling channel, is worth listening to or using yourself. Once hailed on channel 11, the custom is for new contacts to agree to meet with you on another frequency. Channel 9 is the national emergency frequency. It can get pretty dramatic just listening to it. You may also get clues as to the location of police and emergency vehicles. No use flying low past every overworked patrolman in your area, as they are picking up pieces.

We should touch upon "gray" broadcasts, sometimes said to be made by police officers to entrap drivers. Evidence is good that this has been, and is being done, but principally in areas already famous for speed traps. Still, be careful of "road clear — no Smokeys" reports that differ from the pattern you have been hearing on your monitor. Your own copy of FCC Section 95 will make the illegality clear: (S/95.115) *No person* shall transmit false or deceptive communications by radio, or identify the station he is operating by means of a call sign which has not been assigned to that station."

It is often hard to prove one has been victimized in this way. In areas where this is a favorite trick, try tape recording several deceptive calls and getting together with others who were taken in. It could provide enough grounds for legal counteraction. Even if you cannot save yourself from a traffic conviction, be sure to report your suspicions to the FCC. There may be a conspiracy investigation already developing in your area.

Practical Range

Maximum peak envelope power for all legal CB AM class D transmitters is 4 watts. Under ideal conditions, a mobile unit operating at top efficiency, with a well mounted high-performance antenna, can get out about twenty miles over flat country - perhaps a little more over water or marsh. As a practical matter, you may expect to get out ten miles down the road if terrain is flat earth or sloping away from you. To be really safe, you must discount all but extremely high-performance installations down even further. Most inexpensive sets, radiating through antenna mounts which are necessarily in compromise locations, will send strong signals out about three miles over the longest lobe of their signal pattern, and a little over one and a half miles over the opposite-facing, foreshortened lobe. This will be amplified when we discuss antenna selection and installation.

Now - how does this apply to the detection and frustration of Smokey's intentions? Remember, we have established the optimum radar acquisition range as around 1,000 feet from your oncoming car. This means that, at worst, a good samaritan up the line with only a mediocre setup, can get word back toward you at least five times further than Smokey can reach with even the best radar setup. If you are passed by a patrol car on a high-speed sweep, you may, under similar circumstances, be able to warn listeners three to six minutes ahead of you and Smokey. This has the effect of multiplying the bears' presence, but reducing the number of tickets - actually promoting an extremely efficient traffic flow.

Equipment Selection

There will be a set price area for most of us. Within that price range, you will be surprised how much variation there is in specifications of transceivers and scanners. When you consider possible choices by reading ads, catalogs, magazine reports or consulting CB shops, it is best not to buy any unit without comparing the top six specifications. Generally valued as the most important criteria in judging the worth of radio equipment, these are: output power; sensitivity; selectivity; spurious rejection; modulation, and audio output. All other features are accessory devices related to noise suppression and fine tuning. Actually, the better these top six circuits, the less you need the hand controls.

The Specs:

Output power is often the first item examined by a prospective buyer, in much the same way a car enthusiast might scan the specs for "zero to sixty" acceleration time. In fact, a transceiver power rating of 2.5 watts is just about as strong in transmission as a full 4 watts. The peak envelope power rating is the most important figure, and is more dependent on your antenna system's standing wave or signal power ratio. The antenna section will tell you how to check and compute your exact PEP rating.

Sensitivity is of basic importance. It is the prime measurement of your CB's ability to receive signals. The spec is usually written as: "X uV for 10 dB." The smaller the quantity "X," the better. A 1 uV or less rating is common among the middle priced sets.

Spurious rejection refers to the transmitter's consistency in staying on a desired channel. A high number of at least over forty dB is needed.

Modulation is related to the percentage of transmitter power actually in use. The closer your transmitter power is to 100 percent rating, the better you will be understood by other CB'ers.

Audio output of your transceiver's speaker, or remotely connected speakers, can be critical under noisy driving conditions. A rating of one watt for an in-set speaker is adequate, but the sign of a more expensively built set is the ability to get closer to 6 watts.

There is much talk about extra tuning features in some of the units. Many of these are fast becoming standard on the better sets, and all are desirable. They include the automatic noise limiter, blanker (silencer), delta tuning, signal-radio frequency output meter, standing wave ratio meter, and talk power booster. The effectiveness of all such accessory circuits is hard to judge without listening to or transmitting over a unit already mounted in a vehicle similar to yours. Those CB shops which have a number of demos set up in-house may be valuable if using mobile antennae, and if in use in the same geographical area in which you plan to do your driving — a lot of ifs.

The extra tuning features:

The **ANL** switch is for suppressing engine and electrical system noises. It is usually coupled with a **blanker,** which uses other circuits to work against outside atmospheric disturbances.

Delta tuning takes advantage of your set's selectivity by "hunting" a little to one side of a true frequency to bring in distorted signals. So many mobile sets are not tuned well for all frequencies that this fine tuning is useful for catching that one tiny voice which may tip you off that Smokey is hiding over the hill. Quite a few users simply mount and connect components without doing a final antenna PEP tuneup. This is why we consider three miles a more realistic dependable sending and receiving range for over-the-road communications.

S/RF Meters show relative signal strengths when you are receiving or sending. Receiving mode usually shows a range of one to nine units of reception strength in an abstract numbering. In transmitting mode, a good quality set's RF reading should be calibrated in true watts. Some less expensive sets show only another graduated scale of abstract numbers or zones, from which you must estimate watt output. The incoming signal strength reading is a good indicator of distance between yourself and the sender. The higher the reading, the closer he is to you. If it goes off the scale, he is right behind or ahead of you.

A **SWR meter** indicates the condition of your antenna system. Only in the most expensive sets will you have a really accurate SWR calibration when it is a built-in. For all antenna tuning, you will still be using a separate SWR meter connected in-line for PEP calculations.

Talk power boosters are more likely to be offered on a set as you go a bit farther up the price ladder. This is a circuit that boosts that part of the signal containing your voice. The practical effect is to make your voice more audible for a greater distance than the identical set without a voice booster.

Linear Amplifiers

Although not legally adapted to any CB or single side band transceiver, the linear amp is a fact of CB life. You have heard them called "boots," or perhaps "foot-warmers." Their sole use is to increase transmitter power.

The mobile linear is the device that brings you a report from a trucker twenty-five miles down the road. It is the same device that enables you to switch on an extra, 10, 20, — commonly up to 100 — extra watts, in order to query that same trucker on channel 19 for more details on Smokey's latest VASCAR zone. You and the trucker, occasionally operating "with boots on" while out on the open road, are the safest of all linear amp users. Understand that we do not advocate the use of illegal power outputs, and we have already made the point that normal minimum outputs will give you plenty of warning time. Still, the linear amp, all the way up to a "full gallon," (1,000 watts!), is a reality in CB operation. It is predicted that sooner or later the linear will become legal for Class D use, but not in the near future.

Why, you may ask, are linear amps available at all, if illegal for CB? The reason is that they have been sold for years as a legal accessory for ham radio gear. There they are, right on the shelf in the electronics store, with the CB gear. It is not against the law to sell them to anyone. Some stores take the attitude that it is not even illegal to install one in your car, if the amp is yours and not theirs. Since most linears are usable over a broad range of frequencies, from 3 to 30 MHz for example, and CB falls into 26 to 27 MHz, who knows why you are buying it?

There are a number of different types of linear amps. The most common is probably the bi-linear, which works on both incoming signals and transmission. The practical effect is to improve your hearing on one end and put your signal out a multiple of your original radius, still dependent on your antenna's capability. Some linears act on incoming signals only, and these are perfectly legal for CB use. A few little black boxes are so small and discreet that they are obviously for use only on outgoing signals. These are sometimes connected to auto accessory toggle switches labelled "defroster," or other innocuous term.

Linears are not cheap, although they are very easy to install. A good one, in the vicinity of 100 extra watts, is as much as a medium priced CB. Some will work on single side band as well as AM/CB. With 12 watts of SSB power, (single side band is legally limited to 12 watts), you will have about as much long range capability as the President's yacht! But, beware. The FCC monitors around the clock, looking for transmissions with excessive power. Most users of amps keep the power burst short, and, sadly, seem to forget their call signs. By the way, since Uncle Charley (the FCC) patrols at least as hard at night as during the day, do not be lulled into false security because you use an amp only for the long, fast night runs.

Should you own a linear amplifier? You probably will not need it to foil speed traps. Yet, in an emergency, being able to shout for help five times further away might make a difference. That is one time when you would be glad to hear from the FCC.

Installation of Transceivers

Unfortunately, one has to consider the risk of theft when installing electronic gear. Some units will fit entirely behind a dash or glove compartment door. Other units, at greater cost, may be had which permit all but a microphone-mounted control head to be set up under the seat or in the trunk. Any arrangement that allows the CB and other components to be kept out of sight, including an antenna which disappears or is easily removed, is recommended. It is a pity this is necessary, because such installations decrease the unit's performance to some extent. However, insuring for CB scanner loss is becoming almost impossible.

An arrangement which is almost as desirable is the in-dash mount. Several makers produce combination sets offering CB/AM/FM, and even cassette music and recording, miniaturized into an apparently normal dash fitment. Not cheap, but hard to steal. Read specs carefully when considering these, as some have CB circuits on the low performance side. When coupled with compromised antenna installations, over-the-road performance from such do-all sets suffers. In urban areas, however, these are a good arrangement.

The easiest to install, and also the easiest to steal, are sets with simple, sheet metal brackets. You must be willing to remove the set from its thumbscrews every time you leave your car — a practice most people soon give up. You can be sure that it is the antenna that attracts attention. Then, if your set is in a simple under-dash bracket, your poor car will be ravished with a coathanger and the CB and/or scanner removed in as little as two minutes.

In the absence of inexpensive CB theft insurance, a car alarm is itself cheap insurance. A window sticker proclaiming an auto alarm system, furnished with some anti-theft systems, is almost as great a deterrent as the device itself. The CB thief will simply look for greener pastures, as the industry estimates that only about one quarter of all car-mounted electronics have been alarm safeguarded.

The Antenna

We have talked a lot about radio range, because the stronger your send/receive capability, the harder it will be for Smokey to trap you. By now, it should be obvious that your choice and location of an antenna is at least as important as your choice of two-way radio. A car owner is often very picky about his choice of CB or SSB, and yet may be uncertain which antenna to get, because each antenna is highly individual. It is not uncommon for a poor antenna installation to reduce a good CB's range from five to ten miles down to two or three. All antennae have drawbacks under the compromise condition necessary to an automobile or truck installation. In general, we want good reception and transmission under high speed conditions.

Peak Envelope Power

To get average performance from your radio, you must use an antenna system that gives a signal wave ratio of not over 1:2. This is ascertained by attaching an SWR meter between the transceiver and antenna transmission line. On most antenna, there is a "load" adjustment which you can manipulate to provide the lowest possible SWR reading on the meter. The closer you get to a 1:1 ratio, the more PEP your set has.

It figures this way: If your SWR meter reads 1.5:1, and your rated power is a full 4 watts, divide 4 by 1.5 to get actual PEP. In this case, it would be 2.667 watts. This, by the way, is a very common reading, and many well performing CB's are on the air with 2 to 3 watts of PEP.

Type of Antenna

A whip antenna receives along its entire length, but will only transmit from the bottom two feet, nearest its ground plane. That is why it kills your sending power to put a whip antenna on the rear bumper. The higher the ground plane, in our case the vehicle's roof, the greater the transmission range. However, a roof-mounted, 108 inch antenna would be undesirable to most road users, so whip antennae were long ago superceded by "loaded" antennae. Some of these are as short as three and a half feet, and have a long coil of wire somewhere within them (at the base, middle, or top) to make up the signal radiation distance of 108 inches (one quarter wavelength). There are scores of makers competing for your mobile antenna dollar with these convenient "loaded" units.

Location

In general, a good location for all our purposes is the trunk lid, or in the quarter panel just to the passenger side of it. When the antenna is placed here, it radiates its best patterns ahead toward the driver's side and beyond and, to a somewhat lesser extent, backward toward traffic in your lanes. Switching to the front cowling ahead of the windshield is also all right, especially if the hood's ground plane slopes slightly away downward toward the road. It is very important to locate and silence all engine electrical interference when the antenna is mounted at the front in this way.

Mounting

As previously mentioned, any antenna is an invitation to CB thieves. So, security considerations also govern antenna choices and locations. Antennae that fold out of the way or retract electrically or remove and store easily, are all more theft-proof than large, semi-permanent types. However, all anti-theft units lose a little performance because they are short, made in sections, or prone to flexing when the vehicle is moving. Among these, a good bet is the magnetic rooftop mounted antenna, which is meant to be easily removed and stored away. The most convenient, and the most expensive, is the motorized disappearing unit with a tunable top load.

Duals

Many trucks use dual antennae, called "co-phased." Because of this, many car drivers have purchased them also. On a large truck, when the two antennae can be spaced over 100 inches apart, they help signals in and out around the cargo van. On a standard auto, where 100 inch offset is not possible, they are a waste of money in most cases. In the future, manufacturers may have dual antennae for autos that provide some gain in efficiency, but none are presently on the market.

Sunspots

The year 1978 will mark the beginning of an eleven year sunspot cycle. It is said that this will change the usefulness of CB radios drastically for the worse. In fact, the U.S. Department of Commerce's Office of Telecommunications recently stated, "CB radios will be nearly useless for several years, for their intended purpose, which is directional short-range communications." Other authorities deny that CB's will be useless, but agree that there will be much more difficulty in managing over-the-road anti-bear intelligence reports.

C.B. QUIZ
☑check one

The scientific explanation for sunspot skip has to do with the various layers of our planet's atmosphere. A turbulent condition on the surface of the sun causes ultraviolet waves to be generated in large quantities.

The main effect of sunspots is to cause radio signals in the 15 to 40 MHz range to begin bouncing far away from the transmitter. Initially in the projected cycle, the effect occurs mainly at night. The effect is similar to, but not the same as, the well-known "skip" effect which occurs at night in many localities. Linear amplifiers discussed elsewhere in this book, are often used to work skip. (This, by the way, is held as illegal on CB by the FCC.) The sunspot skip may send your signals 400 to 1,000 miles away, but in a totally unpredictable manner. The problem lies in your inability to keep in touch five miles down the road, because several calls on the same frequency are bouncing in from across the country with as much strength as if they were transmitting from within one mile.

By 1979, this problem will also be consistent during daylight hours, although you should be able to hold calls down to a mile or so with some success. The effect will be most prominent during fall, winter, and spring of each year. This may be a blessing, as most of us do a lot of fast distance driving during the summer vacation season.

Will CB be obsolete until 1989? No, but your mobile installations will have to operate at top efficiency for all possible short-range signal strength. Radio traffic is less likely to be heavy on the open road, so a little dial scanning should turn up a clear channel for bear bulletins. On frequencies like 9, 11, and 19, there may be a lot of skip jamming. In the future, the truckers, emergency response networks and others will probably agree on alternate hailing and reporting channels in case the primary frequencies are blocked. There are, after all, up to forty channels available.

The FCC is entertaining the idea of opening up a new citizens' band of frequencies called Class E. This lies in the 50 MNz to 100 MHz sector, and is relatively sunspot-proof. However, commercial broadcasting networks (ABC, NBC, and CBS), as well as ham radio enthusiasts, have already served notice that they will fight it. Without going into detail here, it may be said that each has some grounds of concern.

Single Side Band

What can a mobile radio user do to counteract sunspot interference? There are three possibilities: Obtain a ham radio license, install a high-power linear amplifier, or purchase and use a single side band transceiver. Of these, the last is perhaps the most practical. It requires considerable study to pass the ham test, and you would probably not want to do this simply to have the capability of out-communicating Smokey. The linear amp is, of course, quite illegal for CB. Its effect would be to extend your line-of-sight communications ability by perhaps several miles, but your own skip would be coming in over the Dalai Lama's aquarium bubbler in the Himalayas.

Finally, there is single side band transmission. SSB actually transmits over the same wavelengths as CB, but with greater power and clarity. One could say that is has the same effect as a mild linear amplifier; but single side band is legal. With SSB at twelve watts PEP, you can hope for some fifty miles extreme range, with a practical range in excess of twenty-five miles. The main drawback is cost, although there may soon be a big demand for low-priced SSBs. Right now, a forty channel SSB will cost several hundred dollars.

A different form of license and call code is required for SSB, although it is as legal as CB standard mode. So many fewer users own SSB that there is far less traffic on the SSB call channel 16. Once a conversation is started, the two speakers go on to an unused channel, where they have no standard AM/CB or SSB interference. This is called going "QSO." A listener on standard CB will be able to hear, but not understand, an SSB transmission on their channel. However, the SSB user can understand all CB transmissions, as well as SSB. This means that SSB blocks out regular CB signals the same way that a CB user does. In most locations, SSB users conduct clear-channel calls on only a few of the forty available channels. Then, they either switch to a quiet SSB channel or go to CB mode, as most SSB sets can be switched back to regular CB channel.

At present, SSB is legally limited to twelve watts peak envelope power. This is, of course, three times the max CB rating. All other things being equal, the same efficiency of antenna setup will drive clear SSB transmissions three to four times further. This is ideal for preserving longer range over-the-road communications. The SSB skips out the same was as CB does, but, for the next few years, there will be far less air traffic on the channel 24 through 40 SSB. Therefore, there will be less interference on SSB. A linear amplifier would also have the same effect of increased power on a SSB as on a ham or CB radio.

The upshot is that using one or more of these three methods, sunspots or no, you will still be able to reach out close to the ten mile marker on the road ahead, although it will cost you some extra study, money or risk.

Chapter VI
Police Transmissions and Scanners

There are several reasons why you might want to have a monitor in your car which would pick up local or statewide police transmissions. Foremost of these is that you would be able to pick up bulletins regarding road conditions ahead. Probably a close second is that you would have a channel always set to your region's Federal Weather Service broadcasts, which are constantly updated. Of course, you may be a police buff, a hobbyist with a sympathetic interest in the trials and tribulations of police work. We have heard of a few cynical souls who keep a scanner set to state and local highway patrol frequencies, because they might some day want to know who and how many are one bend back or one hill ahead of them.

Police Radio Nets

States with far-flung road nets supply their highway patrols with radio systems that have numerous "repeaters"; that is, antenna/receiver/rebroadcast units mounted on high vantage points all over the state. In most cases, there is at least one frequency allocated to statewide communications between all highway patrol units in range of each other, or a repeater frequency. Most states also have a statewide law enforcement mutual aid channel, with both a base and a relay setup.

Should you be one mile ahead in a five mile race to a freeway exit, you would have, perhaps, two minutes to hear your scanner pick up transmissions on all the above mentioned frequencies, as the pursuing officer reported the situation to his dispatcher, and the base station sent out messages to other highway patrol units. You might also have the pleasure of hearing another mobile unit replying to your pursuer, regarding pulling a U turn across some convenient stretch of centerstrip and getting a handle on you. As an added stimulus, your scanner might pause briefly on the all services assistance repeater channel, and hear how local law was being enlisted to wait at some or all exit ramps you might choose to use.

Transmissions like that might make you sweat a bit, but they would provide valuable intelligence. You could conceivably pull your own U turn, bearing in mind the hazards you might cause innocent parties, short of the location of an intercepting patrol car. You would certainly know instantly if the officer had been able to spot your license plate before you put your foot through the floor.

Unless you are the felonious type, these will be extremely rare circumstances. Ordinarily, you will simply stop and accept a citation, using the methods outlined in this book for ameliorating the seriousness of the ticket, and later reducing or quashing the conviction in traffic court. Still, Smokey's radio net is what really puts a firm foundation under his radar set and we ought to examine it closely. Less dramatic, but more useful, is the fact that his communications often reveal where he is and what he is doing.

Police radio systems operate on VHF and UHF frequencies, with greater power allowed by the FCC. As a rule, expect the bears to be able to talk among themselves for as many as fifty miles along long, flat roadways. There will at times be "dead" areas wherein a mobile unit cannot reach base, and a repeater is blocked from reaching other mobiles, but these areas will be rare and kept secret.

Scanner Intelligence

We have already alluded to some of the information you can acquire by monitoring police channels. When you know the roadway yard by yard, you can get the most out of police transmissions. Should there be spots along the way that indicate difficulty in sending or receiving highway patrol transmissions, you might file the information away for future reference. Reconnoiter your most traveled routes and scan the bands. What do truckers say about police tactics? What does Smokey say to other bears? You cannot know too much about an area where you might have to practice tactical thinking. You may be sure that Smokey has expert help in setting up his contingency plans for road chases, interceptions, and placement of speed monitoring devices.

The Frequencies

You know you can buy many models of scanner, but how do you know what channel Smokey is on? You will have up to sixteen frequencies that you can monitor, depending on the expense of your scanner. Most compact mid- and low-priced scanners are eight to ten channel units.

We set our eight channel scanner up with the California Highway Patrol All Services Statewide channel (42.18 MHz), as well as several local police, fire and mutual aid channels. Also added as channel 8 was the regional Federal Weather Advisory frequency (162.55 MHz). As this is always on the air, remember to lock out the scan on that frequency until you want to check upcoming weather.

The key is to know your local radio traffic well, and choose exactly the crystals or other forms of setting needed for your locality, with some added statewide frequencies. If you are planning a rapid coast-to-coast cruise, then scanning becomes something of a problem. To handle police call monitoring over several states, you must review all lists for as many common frequencies as possible. Then, as you leave one jurisdiction and enter another, you will have to pull a coffee stop and replace some crystals or other adjustments with new ones. Since good quality crystals may cost from five to ten dollars, this can quickly run into money, but it is part of the price of eternal vigilance.

Several annual booklet services are available that give every listed channel in use under FCC regulation, which includes all police, fire, local government, emergency services, ambulances, county coroners, and many more which are not particularly germane to fast driving.

The largest series of booklets is probably *Police Call*, with volumes covering every region of the U.S. These lists are sold for about five dollars, and are well worth it if you are going to invest in a scanner. (Write: *Police Call*, Dept. T, Lebanon, N.J. 08833). The experimental scanner set for this book was equipped with crystals selected from the pages of the Southern California detail edition of *Police Call*, edited by Gene C. Hughes. Even if you do not live in Southern California, the background information regarding police transmission is excellent.

At the top of the scanner price lists come those with more convenient methods of programming frequencies. Some use electro-opticals, others are semicomputerized. With these, you can make a cross-country run without missing many necessary frequencies. However, you will pay well for the convenience, and the thought of having one of these ripped off is enough to cause headaches.

In strange territory, without knowledge of, or ability to, monitor the appropriate channels, rely more on the trucker channel and other CB/SSB bear bulletins.

Tactical Frequencies

Those who already have public service band scanners may wonder about tactical frequencies. Remember on "Adam 12," how the base dispatcher sometimes advises Reed and Malloy that "the detectives will meet you on tac 2?" The same situation might one day apply, if highway patrol units bent on intercepting you agree to meet on a tactical frequency that is scrambled. This may especially be the case if pursuing officers suspect that you are equipped with a police scanner.

Locating a crystal for any police department's tac frequencies is not the problem. They are listed in the directories with all the others cleared by the FCC. Unscrambling them is another matter. Bear in mind that any use of a radio intercept for personal gain, in any way whatsoever — whether it is our hypothetical anti-ticket race or countersurveillance during a bank robbery — is a federal offense. A lot of people are going to be upset that we have even mentioned it.

Unscrambling

Once you have decided to add unscrambling ability to your PSB monitor, you only have to look in the classifieds of the mechanics, electronics, and auto enthusiast magazines. There, you will find listings offering descrambler circuits, kits, and ready-made add-on units. These run in the vicinity of forty dollars each, ready to go, and makers like Information Unlimited, Box 626, Lord Jeffey Place, Amherst, N.H. 03031, will assure you of the correct crystals and chips to unscramble one or more tac channels used in your own locale. No doubt they use the same frequency lists we do and then program the inversions from there.

You should have a basic understanding of how police scramblers work. Most of them are relatively simple, although the presence of greater public access will begin driving police departments into more and more sophisticated methods of secrecy.

The usual method of low priority secret telephone and simple police department tactical frequency scrambling is called speech inversion. There are far more advanced voice encoding devices, but these are usually expensive, and unnecessary for information of a quickly perishable value. At the upper end of the secrecy scale are the State Department, CIA, and presidential transmissions that are done in rolling code band splitters. These cannot be broken without the expert use of electronic equipment and an analog computer of some size. In between lie commercial encoding, military field communications, and certain police departments that have managed to raise their budgets to obtain more sophisticated communications security. These last usually get the price of better scramblers only after demonstrating that well-equipped felons were listening in on their Speech Inversion. These mid area methods of scrambling include frequency hopping inverters and ban splitters.

Let us return to speech inversion, the simplest of the methods, the one most commonly used by police departments, and the only one we are going to discuss. When we say speech inversion, we mean just that. On tactical frequencies, one or two high-pitched sounds are transposed to low, and vice versa. At the normal speed of speech, the inversions are not usually intelligible to unskilled listeners. Yet, it is reported that, since some overseas telephone calls have been in the form of inverted signals since World War II, experienced operators have become able to mentally decipher simple scrambled messages well enough to comprehend the meaning of phrases.

Rather than try that, we might simply send for the hobby kit that provides us with a circuit containing a device called a ring modulator, and a circuit for generating audio tones between 1,000 and 10,000 Hz. In some cases, the exact frequency is preset by the maker, according to your order or his own knowledge of tac channels in your area. In other cases, a more universal unit is sold, which allows you to tune the audio signal generator across the modulation of the inverted signal. When the frequencies are correctly paired, the inversion of the scramble becomes audible. This is, of course, normal speech once again.

Budget conscious readers who are handy with a soldering iron should not despair. Go to the library and Xerox the March, 1970 article in *Popular Electronics,* which describes methods of unscrambling both radio and telephone speech inversion with a home-built outfit.

Chapter VII
Police Cars - How to Spot Them

If eternal vigilance is the price of freedom from traffic tickets, then the first principle of vigilance is the rapid identification of police cars.

Because a small rearview mirror weighs only a few ounces, because gold is worth about a hundred dollars an ounce, and because traffic tickets cost dearly, it is not unreasonable to say that a rearview mirror is worth its weight in gold. In order to spot police cars before they become a menace, you must both see and identify them. This chapter provides some useful guidelines.

What is a Police Car?

Police cars come in many packages, but the vast majority are from Chrysler and General Motors. While there are many differences between these makes, there are even more similarities.

Among the packages available to police departments, the state patrols generally choose cars that are faster and better equipped for high speed pursuit than those purchased by city departments. Both used to buy only full-size, four-door vehicles, but since the gas crunch we are seeing some city police in something less than full-size models. Dodge Darts are not uncommon, nor are intermediate-sized Chevrolets like the Nova. Motorcycles, years ago the nemesis of the highway speeder, are now primarily relegated to city traffic.

A police vehicle must be capable of operating efficiently in all temperatures and road conditions, must be capable of some off-the-road use, and some high-speed cruising and maneuverability. It needs adequate electrical power for the multitudinous accessories, and must not overheat, even after hours of roadside idling. All in all a pretty big order. Some of these requirements are fulfilled better than others.

Basically, the difference between the police car and the ordinary passenger car is the presence of various elements of heavy-duty equipment on the police car. This difference is more marked than the power increasing engine modifications, although most police cars have them, especially the highway patrol cars. These heavy-duty features include the frame, front and rear suspension, front stabilizer bar, transmission, brake linings, cooling system, battery, and even the seats. Wider rims and heavy-duty wheels often complete the picture.

Ford offers four police packages, available in several of their full-size models, and even in hardtops and station wagon models. In the order of increasing horsepower and handling modifications, these are the Sentinel, the Guardian, the Cruiser, and the Police Interceptor. Although Ford no longer publically announces their horsepower, cubic inch displacement (200 to 460 cubes) would indicate a range from about 155 up to perhaps 240 horsepower. The Police Interceptor package probably has even more horsepower. This is the maximum duty vehicle, capable of sustained high speed for highway and freeway pursuit. This model is essentially a souped up Cruiser with a high lift cam, improved carburetion, modified manifolds, dual exhausts, balanced crankshaft, and heavy-duty connecting rods and oil pump.

Chevrolet also offers patrol cars in several current sedan models and wagons. Equipped with essentially the same heavy-duty features as Ford's, wrapped around three basic engine types, they range in displacement from 250 to 454 cubes, developing from 165 to 225 horsepower.

Chrysler provides police cars in Dodge and Plymouth models. At present there are more Chrysler-made police cars in the United States than any other kind, and they expect to sell about 35,000 law enforcement vehicles in 1977. These vehicles range in engine size from 360 to 440 cubes, with a range of power from 170 to 245 horsepower. Most of the police engines have various carburetion options that will increase power in a particular engine size.

Let us take a close look at one of the classic examples, the 1977 Dodge Monaco Police Pursuit, which is in widespread use throughout the U.S. This vehicle will go from 0 to 60 miles per hour in 8.1 seconds and devour a quarter mile in 16.3 seconds. The acceleration between 60 and 90 miles per hour is bodacious, with a top speed peak out of around 126 miles per hour.

A peek under the hood reveals the secret - 440 cubes of V-8 with special connecting rods and bearings, a shot-peened nodular cast-iron crankshaft, hot-pressed valve dampers, a lubrite treated camshaft, double roller timing chain, chrome flashed exhaust valve stems, and thick wall exhaust manifolds venting through dual exhausts - all this fired by silicon insulated ignition wiring through an electronic ignition system, and fed by a four barrel carburetor. To cool this hot setup, you will find a large capacity radiator, a coolant recovery system, and a seven bladed fan. The Torque-flite automatic transmission is equipped with an oil cooler, and there is a power steering pump cooler. This package boosts out a husky 350 foot pounds of torque, and is rated at 245 horsepower.

How do they keep it on the road? The answer is revealed by a look underneath - larger shock absorbers, heavy-duty front torsion bars, heavy-duty front and rear anti-sway bars, heavy-duty rear springs. Torsional stiffness is assured by extra welds and inner panel reinforcement of the unit body.

Sooner or later, somebody has to stop this piece of guided steel. That feat is accomplished by a dual tandem, diaphragm power booster activating heavy-duty semi-metallic disc pads on the front, and by a pair of drum brakes in the rear, acting on Seventy-Series Goodyear Police Special fabric radials. This combination provides a 209 foot (0.78G) stop from seventy miles per hour.

A high capacity, 100 ampere alternator charges an 85 ampere hour battery to provide the electricity for radios, radar, VASCAR, lights and other gadgetry.

Out of curiosity, I checked to see if the average citizen could purchase the Chrysler police car options, including the super hot engine, the special handling package, the suspension, shocks, roof reinforcement plate, and even the certified calibrated speedometer to 140 miles per hour. It costs a lot (upwards of $5,700), but everything is available except the siren and badge.

In summary, no matter what the make of any police car you may encounter, you can expect it to be fast, handle well, stop quickly, and be capable of surviving a lot of abuse.

While police cars are available in most colors, characteristically they are black, white, blue, green, or some other unobtrusive color. Most of them have spotlights, but the old waving aerials are gone. Rooftop light fixtures may be of many varieties; anything from single to double, triple, quadruple, or a solid band of light may be seen. Most police cars are currently being equipped with a blue flashing light rather than the old classic red. This innovation was made in order to avoid the competition of red tail lights, stop lights, neon lights, and the like.

Unmarked Cars

A friend of mine, who collects lots of speeding tickets, told me that the only way he knew to spot unmarked police cars was to shine a flashlight in the window and look for a reflection off the badge. Fortunately there are some better methods.

Police cars invariably have telltale license plates. While these vary from state to state, county to county, and city to city, they are characteristic, and you should learn those in your area. City plates often start with the letter M for municipal, but other single or multiple letters may be used in particular cities. County plates often begin with C, and state plates may be S or SP for state police or patrol, or have the letter of the state as a prefix. Because police cars are generally well maintained, a bent or tilted license plate can immediately disqualify the vehicle as a cop car.

Sometimes unmarked cars will have a small identification number on the back window or trunk, but the license plate is more easily seen, and should forewarn you against overtaking an unmarked car.

Spotlights are usually a standard feature on unmarked cars, and help to identify them, as spots are no longer a common feature on passenger cars. Some patrol cars have two mounted spotlights at the front doors, with the red or blue one on the driver's side. The clear one is used to illuminate the interior of a suspicious car, or other site, during a night stop. Some of the recent unmarked cars are sporting a new form of red or blue lamp made by Noren Products, Inc. that appears normal until lit.

Although the amber parking lamps may be small, because emergency visibility is critical, all police vehicles have large, obvious stop lights. Yellow caution lights may be mounted behind the rear window.

Occasionally you will see the silhouette of a dash-mounted flashing light, but many of these cars conceal the light behind the front grill. The other common location for flashing lights is mounted in one or both of the front dual headlamp inner sockets.

Even the unmarked cars usually have facilities for locking prisoners in the back seat. Although this is commonly glass and not readily visible, you will notice that there is a piece of steel grating on each side to prevent prisoners from reaching around into the front seat. This grating is often visible, marking the car for what it is.

Light coming through a leading or trailing car's windshield helps with the silhouette checking. You may even spot the radar antenna itself, mounted inside or near the car's rear door at a window frame or roof rain gutter. It looks like a two foot by six inch horn or megaphone, made of nonreflective black fiberglass on a chromeplated mounting bracket. Now and again you may spot a dash-mounted riot shotgun fastened butt upright on the floor. It looks like a black one inch pipe rising about three inches above the dash in the midpoint of the front seat.

Highway pursuit cars, whether marked or unmarked, usually sit lower on their suspensions and use somewhat wider tires than do the standard cars. Dual exhaust pipes are the rule.

Actually, there are more indications to eliminate your suspect as a police car than to identify it. For example, since the long police aerial is gone, a car with a long aerial is not a police car; more likely, it belongs to a ham radio operator. Somewhere on the police car is a small VHF whip antenna, but if you are close enough to see this, it may be too late.

Police cars, even unmarked, are usually of solid colors and not gaudy, so you can eliminate reds, yellows, color two-tones, and also convertibles, compacts, foreign cars, and makes not used for police work. In the last year, though, I have seen a couple of uncharacteristic colors in my state, so take note of what your state is using. This is accomplished by noting what type of car has pulled over the speeder or by cruising past your local city, county, or state police stations. You will not see anything dangling from mirrors or stuck onto aerials, unusual lights, or other gimmicks. Plain is the rule. But - plain cherry looking. Police cars are subject to thorough routine maintenance, so dirt is quickly washed off, and dents, scrapes, and missing hubcaps are quickly repaired or replaced.

More than one person in the car generally eliminates the possibility of state police, because they usually work alone. However, there are exceptions in some states, California included. Most large cities routinely place two officers in their patrol cars. Of course, you could get caught up in a situation in which a state cop is training a rookie, but you are playing an odds game.

Police hat silhouettes are occasionally telltale, some areas even using crash helmets, but many police remove their hats while driving to avoid this giveaway. At any rate, you can eliminate anyone with really long hair, male or female.

A few states (Massachusetts is one) allow certain of their traffic police to use their own cars, trucks, or vans for traffic control. The state pays a mileage and upkeep allowance. These vehicles, of course, are totally unpredictable in appearance, but still often have some of the features heretofore mentioned.

Some other states allow their officers to use the police cars when off duty. Their rationale is that it helps to increase the public's sense of "officer presence." Although an off duty policeman is not likely to stop anyone but the most flagrant violator, he does have the capacity for radioing ahead to police on duty.

A final important method of identification is noting the way the police drive. This is discussed at the end of this chapter.

Night Spotting

In many ways, spotting police cars at night is easier than in the daytime. Noticing license plates should keep you from inadvertently passing an unmarked car during the night as well as in the day, and several other tips which apply to the identification of unmarked cars are valuable at night in a silhouette situation: for example, the spotlight, single driver, and lack of dangling objects.

The key to night spotting, however, is awareness. When I am on the highway at night, I know every car I have passed. Just as in bridge or poker, it is essential to know which cards, or in this case, which cars are in play. I come upon a car, identify it, overtake it, and move on to the next, but always remembering it in my rearview mirror. A new car appearing on the scene must be identified before speed can be resumed.

If the suspect car has dim or unequal headlights, which is quite a common ailment, he is automatically eliminated as a shark. Most police vehicles have well-charged batteries, and their lights are frequently checked and balanced during routine maintenance. Other cars eliminated are those with lights low and/or close together (foreign cars or compacts), and those with lights high and/or wide apart (trucks).

Perhaps you never gave it much thought, but most police cars have a characteristic face at night. This is determined by where and what kind of headlights are used and their relationship to the parking or running lights. Headlights may be single or dual. If dual, they can be either vertically or horizontally placed. Parking lights can be above, below, to the outside, or to the inside of the headlights. A prime example of this detection method: I perceived in 1972 that virtually every highway or freeway police vehicle of that year, whether it was a Ford, Chevrolet, or Chrysler product, had dual headlights with amber parking lights lit *below* the headlights. That year it was like playing with a marked deck.

In most states, highway patrol cars are purchased by the fleet at about three year intervals. In states where weather and anti-ice preparations are hard on a car, it is closer to two years. Since most police cars travel close to 100,000 miles a year, it is not often you find old ones. Even with excellent preventive maintenance, most are replaced before 200,000 miles are logged. Consequently, you only have to memorize the faces of current models.

Games the Bears Play

It may initially surprise you when I suggest that police drive in such a characteristic manner that you can frequently spot them. But, after I point out a few examples, you will see what I mean. This knowledge has frequently saved me from tickets, especially at night.

As we have pointed out, police cars are usually high powered vehicles capable of rapid acceleration, especially at speed. This very power often helps you pick them out of a crowd. Watch for *a car behind you covering a particular distance very rapidly.* For example, I remember seeing a car far behind me as I prepared to climb a long hill. When I was a couple of blocks past the top of the hill, I could see the flash of headlights approaching the crest. I immediately slowed, knowing that the chance of a standard vehicle covering that stretch that fast was very slight. The headlights slowed when I came into sight, followed me at the speed limit for a few miles, and I saw it was a police car when it turned off.

At night you will find the police car may *come up fast but not overtake you* as the average car cruising at that speed would. He will stay far enough behind so that his identity remains secret while he clocks you. This observation has spared me several unpleasantries with the law.

Because of its rather extensive suspension modifications, a highway patrol car is conspicious in a corner by its absence of lean. *It corners much flatter* than its unmodified brother.

Police frequently *appear out of nowhere.* If you are cruising along with no cars behind you, or just a couple you have identified as civilians, and another car suddenly appears, watch out. This is especially true if you have not crossed any intersections. Chances are, a cop just came out of hiding or accelerated into the pack. Slow down until identification is certain.

Sometimes in traffic you will find the cop *hiding behind another moving car* to avoid detection. He places his car squarely behind the one in front of him, following closely to try to conceal himself from you while he is tracking your car. You may see his silhouette protruding slightly every now and then from behind the decoy car.

Always *beware of a slowing of the pack.* Many times while cruising a freeway where the vehicles are fairly evenly distributed, I will suddenly become aware of a slowing of part of the group. This invariably occurs when a police vehicle mingles with other cars. The average motorist immediately slows, even if he is not exceeding the speed limit.

Another indication is the way police *proceed in unlikely directions,* that is, they often ramble, either while hunting, or in an effort to confuse you. For example, they may come from the north, go a mile or so, and turn north again. It helps if you are familiar with the road system in the area. I have had police try to make me believe they were turning off, only to make a quick turn around and be back on my trail. One even put his turn signal on at an intersection at night and then turned off his headlights to convicc me he was no longer behind. Gave me a whale of a good laugh. One of the more common stunts they use is to take the freeway exit ramp, cross the bridge, and come right back on the freeway behind you, having given you a little time to pick up your speed during their absence.

I have been stopped for not using my turn signals during a freeway lane change, even though the nearest car (the police car) was a half mile or more away. Because many police are almost *pathologically concerned with turn signals,* I have often suspected the bears from long range, and subsequently confirmed the fact, when turn signals were used when no other vehicles were in proximity.

Of course, cops have *favorite hiding places.* The classic motorcycle cop behind the billboard has been replaced by the squad car on the edge of the freeway entrance ramp. Whenever you pass such a ramp, grab a look, but also check for a cop a few seconds later. Often they sit on overpass bridges watching for fast cars.

Be sure to watch for police on roads which parallel the freeways. They may track you from an express lane and nab you where the roads merge. I have avoided this problem by turning off before the merger if I find myself being clocked. You can even stop alongside the road for a while. He is not going to back up a block to get you.

Watch for the solitary car parked off the road, usually with engine running (exhaust emitting fumes) and with a view of a particular stretch of road.

On most state highways the squad cars are sufficiently strung out over the state so as to minimize the chances of seeing two close together, and if you spot one you can be somewhat sure of not seeing another for several miles. This does not apply to busy freeways or in the vicinity of overlapping districts.

Most highway patrolmen work within certain county and city jurisdictional districts, ordinarily encompassing no more than a twenty mile strip of interstate. They are not much interested in pursuing you outside of their district, although they have every legal right to do so, so you need not be too concerned when you are within two or three miles of exiting a state or other jurisdictional area.

I should also mention that Smokey tends to hibernate in bad weather, and even at night. You are much more likely to encounter him on bright, sunny days.

If you follow these suggestions, you will find that eventually you will develop a set of reflexes amounting almost to a sixth sense in spotting police.

Chapter VIII
Police Cars - The Evasion

If the reader expects the author to write subsequent books without the shadow of prison bars falling across his manuscript, this had better be a short chapter. Since police cars can be evaded both before the appearance of the flashing light and even sometimes after, this chapter will be so divided.

Before the Flashing Light

Occasionally you will spot a cop tracking you before he has indicated that you are the intended prey, and you will have a few seconds to take evasive action. Once in a great while you can maneuver yourself down a freeway ramp, leaving him stuck in the traffic. If you are not on a freeway, and if your crime is not too heinous, he will sometimes ignore you, if you turn down a side road or even into a driveway as if you are almost home.

At night, if the circumstances are right, it may be possible to do the "car substitution" gambit, which goes something like this: you are boiling along when you spot a car coming up fast from behind, which you tentatively identify as a cop. Rounding a curve or topping a hill, you look for a car to take your place. You might be able to change lanes and slow down, slip in ahead of your pigeon and let him pass you when the police come into view, or turn down a side-road and kill your lights.

A friend of mine witnessed a classic case involving my car. He was walking down the sidewalk one sunny day when he saw me come zipping around a corner in a red Austin-Healey, cover a short straight of way, downshift around a corner and disappear. Next he heard the squeal of tires, saw a police car round the corner, roar down the road and suddenly stop behind a parked red sports car. The officer jumped out, looked around, felt the hood of the parked car, and proceeded to write a ticket which he inserted under the wiper.

Radar traps are never set up so that there are exit ramps or side roads between the clocking car and the arresting, or chase, vehicle. However, there are often several hundred yards of clear road between them. If you know you have been speeding when you pass the parked radar car, you can stop well before the intercept vehicle. This puts the police in the difficult position of trying to reach you with one or the other of their cars. They are certainly not going to walk. If they elect to use the radar car, they have to disrupt their carefully laid trap. If they rely on the intercept car, he has to back up a hundred yards to where you are. The idea is to sit there until he engages another speeder. While this system does not always succeed, neither does it always fail.

After the Flashing Light

Once the flashing light appears you have problems, because, in addition to any other charge, you are toying with a "resisting arrest" citation if you are caught, unless you can convince the officer that you did not know he was after you. If caught, you might try the story that you thought he was on the way to an emergency, and you were trying to get out of his way.

There are very few ways you can lose the police. First you had better be reasonably sure they did not get your license number. But, with the right vehicle, in certain situations, you have a chance. A motorcycle is one way, unless you are dodging another motorcycle. In heavy traffic it is pretty easy to lose a police car just by heading for spaces too narrow for a car to follow. On country roads it is sometimes possible to take to the rough. A cross-country vehicle like a jeep or dune buggy has a little of the same capacity in certain areas.

One day I was rapidly cruising a country road on my motorcycle without a helmet. While I agree that helmets are the smart way to go, I resent laws requiring them. An individual's life should be his own to protect or endanger as he sees fit. At any rate, I passed an oncoming state police car. The officer recognized my infraction, hit his brakes, and spun around to give chase. I headed my bike through an opening in a fence and smilingly bumped off through a pasture, while the officer grimaced at my dust.

In out and out outrunning a police vehicle, a few considerations are essential. In the first place, most police equipment is built for a chase, and there is not much of it that you can outrun with any ease. I have a friend who brags about how he outran a three-wheeled police motorcycle. This, of course, is no feat, as they are designed principally for parking control, and become unmanageable at speeds much over sixty-five miles per hour. It would be unusual to be chased by one in any situation where speed is a factor. He would also have been able to outrun a metermaid on a motorscooter. Trying to outrun other police vehicles is fraught with so much danger to yourself, the police, and others that it is never worthwhile.

I recall a bona fide emergency situation, in which I was streaking across the outskirts of a city. I powered around a jog in the road and up a fairly steep short hill. While downshifting to engage two more corners, I caught a glimpse of something flashing in my rearview mirror. A second look revealed a police car out of control, nearly colliding with a concrete abuttment. I was worried for his life, not to mention taxpayers' property. I negotiated the corners, stopped on the edge of the road, got out of my car, and waited. He roared wildly around the last corner, hit the brakes, and nearly rammed my parked car. I walked over and looked into his window. He was pale as hell and drenched with sweat. I quickly explained my mission, telling him I had almost arrived at my destination. He mumbled something about my needing a police escort, and I thanked him for his concern.

I should explain that unless you just robbed a bank or something, the police will not attempt to curb a speeding car. They will just follow you, lights flashing, siren wailing, until you stop, crash, run out of gas or nerve, or go out of your mind. The pressure of the chase is enormous, especially as you are running most of the risks by going first. If roads are suitable, the police radio ahead and set up a roadblock.

A friend of mine of international racing fame was once cruising at night through eastern Oregon, making very rapid tracks with a modified Porsche. He explained afterwards that he had on several occasions noticed headlights appear behind him, but he had quickly outdistanced them. Coming upon a roadblock some hours later, he stopped and got out to see what the excitement was all about. "Gee, what's going on, fellows?" After this innocent opener, the police monopolized the conversation, as it appeared he had been the reason for the roadblock. Turns out no one can outspeed radio waves.

Chapter IX
The Police Officer

If you carefully follow the suggestions given in this book, your direct contact with the police should be minimal. If, however, you pile up enough miles, you and the Man will occasionally meet, and it will be extremely helpful to know what he is like, as well as a bit of his psychology. This kind of knowledge allowed me to be stopped seven times in succession without being issued a single ticket.

In gathering this information, I wrote a number of police academies, both municipal and state, in order to secure a representative cross section of requirements and training.

When the officer steps out of his car, and we had better start calling him officer at this point, you can expect him to be between twenty-one and fifty years of age. While several police forces accept candidates at twenty years of age, most do not allow him on solitary patrol until he is twenty-one. Police retirement often comes between fifty and sixty years of age, and officers nearing the ends of their terms are generally removed from patrol duty.

Expect him to be fairly tall. While several cities will allow their police to be as short as five feet eight inches, or even five feet seven inches under special circumstances, most state patrols have minimum standards of five feet nine inches, or even six feet without shoes. Do not be intimidated, however. Most departments have a maximum height of six feet six inches, so if you are that tall, you probably will not have to look up at him. It is interesting that in the state of Washington the minimum height for state police is six feet, unless the candidate has a bachelor's degree; then five feet eleven inches is acceptable.

As far as education goes, most city police (Chicago excepted) require a high school diploma or a G.E.D. (General Education Development Certificate). Most state police departments require a high school diploma, although some accept a G.E.D. as equivalent. And there are departments that require two years of college.

The length of police academy training varied widely among different cities and states, but the curriculum is very much the same. The California Commission on Peace Officers' Standards and Training suggests a minimum program of six weeks, but most academy programs seem to be between fourteen and twenty weeks, a few even longer. The state police ordinarily spend more time on high speed or pursuit driving than the city police, and many of the state police have excellent practice facilities. A track I used to race weekends was used by the state police during the week for their high speed training.

In summary, you can expect the average state cop to be somewhat better educated and a bit bigger, and to have a better grasp of pursuit driving than the average city cop. We have purposely neglected county police, because they are usually not involved in traffic control. This is fortunate indeed, as their budgets are usually even lower than their training and education standards. When I was affiliated with a sheriff's department, several of the police cars had interesting peculiarities. In one, the headlights would gradually dim out when the flashing roof light was activated, which made for an extremely challenging chase. Vehicle maintenance in general was very poor.

One of my most annoying encounters with the county police began one night as I turned onto a through street and found myself being followed at an uncomfortable and dangerous proximity by some idiot. I slowed, but he would not pass. I sped up. He sped up, still clinging tenaciously to my rear end. So, checking to make sure nothing was coming, I hung on and stabbed at my brake. He swerved around me to miss my car, putting me in position to return kind for kind. I snapped on my brights and rode his rear bumper. He did not like it one bit, and in fact stopped right in the middle of the road. As I started around him, he jumped out in front of me in his county police uniform, madder than hell. He had been driving his own car. I pulled off on the shoulder and got out, considerably miffed myself. He crouched in front of his headlights, inspecting my driver's license, while I stood to one side waiting for a car to accidentally rearend his and dispatch him into the next county.

As he prepared to get nasty, I felt this was no time for my usual docile approach, and proceeded to itemize his gross errors - dangerous provocation, stopping his car in the road, stepping in front of an unknown vehicle, crouching in front of his own car, as well as a few smaller things. After a bit of conversation, I agreed to leave him alone if he left me alone.

How to Handle Him

It is not uncommon for the first few sentences you utter to set the entire tone of your confrontation and weigh heavily toward the officer's final decision of whether to issue a ticket or a warning. A classic example is the story of the two young women who were stopped by a Colorado State patrolman for a modest excess of speed. He walked over to their car, and the attractive young driver frivolously asked, "Did you stop us to sell us tickets to the Policeman's Ball?" His immediate, unthinking answer, was "Ladies, state patrolmen don't have balls." After a few seconds of speechless embarrassment, he turned abruptly, returned to his patrol car, and peeled rubber into the night.

Because you can seldom expect this kind of luck, and because the police do not usually cooperate by playing straight man, let us apply a bit of logic to our options.

The first thing to remember in most circumstances is that, as the game opens, the officer has all the winning cards. Antagonism or surliness is a sure way to lose whatever chance you have. Most officer's see a lot of this in a day, and a soft-spoken offender is like a breath of fresh air. A bumper sticker can be a big help if its message is something like "Support Your Local Police." But some kinds of stickers lessen your chances, notably those expressing antisocial or very liberal leanings.

Courtesy is of prime importance. I make a habit of always getting out of my car and walking over to the police vehicle. Certain excuses have a reasonable chance of turning the trick, and others are the kiss of death.

Unacceptable Excuses

While the officer appreciates courtesy, he does not dig groveling, pleading or begging. Such an attitude is self-demeaning, and gains you nothing but a quick ticket.

Incredible as it may seem, an excuse sometimes given is that the speeder was unaware that the police were in the area. While perhaps the most honest excuse, you can imagine how much ice it cuts.

Some of the best laughs a policeman can get are from the semi-honest, but no score excuses offered for speeding. Here are examples of a few that were actually used. There was the woman who explained that she had to rush home to breast-feed her baby. There was the guy who was really making tracks to get home before his country-fried takeout chicken got cold. Wife blaming figures prominently. One fellow explained that his back-seat driver wife had fallen asleep and so had failed to warn him of his increasing speed. Another said that he was trying to catch up with his wife in the car ahead to tell her to slow down. There are those of both sexes who use the excuse that they thought the police car was a bandit, rapist, or whatever. Perhaps the most imaginative excuse I have ever heard was from a veteran who blamed his heavy accelerator foot on shrapnel left over from the Vietnam War.

Having a broken speedometer is of no value in the excuse department. The officer is not allowed to ride in your car anyway, so there is no way for him to know if the speedometer is broken or not; and even if it is, the excuse is still not valid.

The most common reason given for speeding is that the speed did not constitute an unsafe condition. Variations of this are that your car is built for speed, that you are an experienced, excellent driver, that the road was clear, traffic sparse, and so on. All of these are ways of saying that the speed limit is wrong for the area, or at least unjust for you. However true they may be, these are unacceptable excuses to an officer, and by citing such reasons for speeding you are admitting that you knowingly and blatantly violated the law. The cop might even remind you that he only enforces the laws you make.

Health excuses are chancy even when legitimate. Recently, while waiting in a doctor's office, I saw a woman enter who was in great pain from a severe kidney infection. In her haste to get help, she had pushed five or ten miles per hour over the legal freeway limit, and was ticketed by a cop who assured her that *he* was saving her life. She fainted from the pain right after telling the story. In many states the law simply requires the driver to be in a condition fit to operate his car safely, and a driver who is unfit for any reason can be penalized. This includes illness, narcotics, tranquilizers, or even lack of sleep.

Acceptable Excuses

If you happen to have an emergency, or even a semi-emergency, it will sometimes provide an acceptable excuse. Examples are rushing home or to a hospital for an injured member of the family, house afire, and so on. If it is bad enough, you may even get a police escort. But, remember the law says that *no one* shall legally exceed the speed limit unless using a siren and/or flashing emergency light in order to warn and safeguard other motorists.

Some years ago one of my fellow sports car racers was on the scene of a city accident where a child was in critical condition. Putting the child in his car, he took off for the hospital with a police escort. In his enthusiasm, he passed the escort and beat the police to the hospital by several minutes. The cops were too embarrassed to complain officially, and we awarded him a trophy at our monthly sports car club meeting.

While we have mentioned that a nonfunctioning speedometer is not an acceptable excuse, there is one related gimmick that has some merit, and I have seen people escape tickets with it. If you have oversized tires on the rear of your car, your speedometer will indicate a speed lower than your actual speed. If you act sufficiently puzzled and finally ask the officer if your snow tires could have thrown off your speedometer, chances are pretty good that he will explain the mystery to you, ask you to take that into consideration in the future, and let you go.

If there were one or more other cars going the same speed as you when you were picked up, be sure to point it out. There is no reason for the police to discriminate against you unless you were leading the pack. Officers are sensitive to this line, and it is even an acceptable courtroom defense.

An excuse that sometimes works is that you were passing a car that obscured the speed limit sign, or that there was no speed limit sign for several miles, or that it was defaced - whatever is believable. But do not lie if the officer can prove you wrong.

Usually the best approach, and certainly the one that has saved me from the most tickets, is the dumb but sincerely sorry technique. An officer is easily antagonized by someone with a courteous but superior attitude, so avoid heavy displays of intelligence. It is acceptable to say you did not realize you were speeding, or that you failed to see the speed limit sign. Using the dumb approach in conjunction with some of the aforementioned excuses is a good idea. It helps if he thinks you are unfamiliar with the road. If your address is fairly close by, you can explain that you were trying a different route home. Explain all this with a certain apologetic stupidity, as if you would never disobey a law knowingly. You would do well to practice this technique, perhaps on your spouse or lover.

Women stopped by traffic police are ticketed less often than men are, perhaps because women have a natural advantage in this area. They are experts at the big-eyed, smiling, sweet, dumb routine. After a party one night, my wife and I left at the same time, in separate cars. She thought it would be fun to beat me home, although nothing like that had been planned or even mentioned. Rapidly covering the last mile before home, she just managed to stay ahead of what she thought was my car, until it turned into a flashing, wailing behemoth. While she was tearfully telling Smokey the truth, I cruised by, glaring at her. He closed his ticketbook and told her, "Forget it, lady, I can see you've got enough trouble."

Bribing

Regarding this subject, let us begin by saying "don't." It is a rather noxious subject, and I do not much like the principle, but as it is a way of life, I would be derelict if I did not provide a few guidelines. Police salaries frequently start low and progress very slowly. While fringe benefits are often quite liberal, you can not carry them home in your pocket. With this preface we will get on with it.

Bribes have probably been occurring since the first Roman made a U turn with his chariot in a U-No-Turno-Zone. Nevertheless, let me immediately point out that you are treading in a rather dangerous area if you are going to play this game, and you should keep a couple of things prominently in mind. The police in some cities and certain parts of the country are amenable to bribes, while in other parts they are not. It would be well to have some idea of the local police in order to stay out of trouble. Of course, even then you could come upon an honest cop, which brings us to the second point. Know exactly what you are going to say, say it, and no more. What you say had better give you a reasonable defense in the event the cop tries to make trouble. For example, at one time I worked for one of the departments of Cook County (Chicago, Illinois). I was stopped by an extremely offensive cop after accidentally making an illegal left turn. After I had been turning there for several months, the sign was unobtrusively planted with a cop hidden nearby. As he wrote the ticket, I told him in a rather malignant tone, "Maybe I can help you out if you ever have to pass through my department." He took this as a threat, which it was, and told me he was arresting me and taking me in. A witness was present, and I repeated what I had said.

"I know what you meant," he answered, infuriated. "But, pay attention to what I said," I smiled. He ticketed me for the illegal turn, and I had it fixed through my department.

Fixing a ticket, even if you know the channels, may cost you more initially than the cost of the fine, but this is usually more than compensated by avoiding the violation on your record and preventing your insurance rates from increasing. I might also mention that the fix must occur early, before the ticket gets involved in the court system. When it hits that level it is too late for any practical maneuvering.

How much should the bribe be? Unlike tipping, bribing has no basic rule, varying with the offense, the area, the cop, and how much

the briber looks as if he is worth. I have seen police bribed in Chicago for as little as a large handful of change, but do not count on that. Also, although it is sometimes tempting, I would not suggest asking an officer for change, if all you have is a fifty or a hundred. I once bribed a Chicago cop who frankly told me that it was not really enough, but that he would accept it this time. He suggested that I carry more money with me in the future.

The trickiest part, of course, is how the bribe is offered. One technique is to hand the policeman your driver's license in a plastic folder with a twenty dollar bill enclosed. If he is receptive he will take it with almost no words exchanged. If he asks about it, you can tell him it is your "emergency money" or something.

Another technique is the dumb one which involves simply asking if there is not some way you can pay the ticket on the spot, without mailing it or going to court, passing yourself off as completely unfamiliar with the proper procedure.

And then there is the little game of betting the officer twenty bucks or more that he is going to give you a ticket. Making bets is not nearly as great a crime as bribery.

Finally, you might consider the approach of sincere repentance, with the expressed wish that you could write a check to the charity of his choice (perhaps the Patrolman's Benefit Fund) rather than contribute to the traffic court. As in fixing a ticket, any of these techniques could also easily cost you more money initially than the fine, but could well be worth it, depending on the circumstances. Ordinarily, the city police are far more receptive than the state police, and let me warn you again: Our advice is not to try it, but if you do, be careful what you say.

Signing the Ticket

After the officer writes a ticket, he will ask you to sign it. This is simply an acknowledgment that you were issued the ticket. Your signature has nothing to do with your guilt or innocence. I mention this to dispel certain rumors, one of which is that it is like signing a confession. At one time there was a prevalent belief that if you did not sign, the offense would not appear on your driving record and/or your insurance record. This is simply not true. If you choose not to sign, the officer has no choice but to take you directly to the traffic judge (usually a justice of the peace) and try you on the spot. This is ordinarily of no help at all.

When He Is

Everyone knows that you can never find a policeman when you

need one. Of course, conversely, it seems that you nearly always find one when you do not want one; but you can predict, to some extent, when the police are most likely to be haunting the roads. You might say that "the police peek when the traffic peaks." Any time there is likely to be an increase in highway traffic, there will inevitably be an increase in police surveillance. This includes all local and national holidays, with particular emphasis on three-day weekends. The beginning and end of all weekends are the most satisfying times for Smokey's appetite, and opening days are also noteworthy: of hunting seasons, county fairs, special tourist attractions, and race days (horse or auto).

You may find the roads more peaceful on the days and weekends immediately following these high intensity police periods when the police departments often have all available men on duty. Bears insist on their free days too.

How Many He Is

This is a question I cannot accurately answer, but I can give you a reference point for working out your own estimation of the number of troopers in your particular state.

In the State of Washington, we have eight hundred Troopers and our population is about 3.36 million. That's one trooper for every 4200 residents. This works out to one trooper for every 80 miles of state highway at the busiest hour and one trooper for every 600 miles during the early morning hours. Your state may have a similar ratio.

It is generally conceded that on the typical Interstate highway there is a radar equipped patrolman every forty miles.

Chapter X
Miscellaneous Offenses

The majority of moving traffic citations appear in the following order of frequency: speeding, driving without a license, failure to stop for signs and lights, violating turn restrictions, negligent driving, and failure to obey restrictive signs.

While it is beyond the scope of this book to discuss them all in detail, several other offenses besides speeding deserve some comment.

Your Rights

With at least thirty million American motorists ticketed or arrested each year for crimes involving their cars, you may well wonder what rights you have. They are well spelled out, because the automobile is the subject of more statutes and cases in U.S. law libraries than any other mechanical object, including the gun.

You do have a legal right to own an automobile - to own one, not to drive one. In every state a driver's license is a privilege, not a right, and is issued on the condition that the state may suspend or revoke it. Repeated violations of minor rules or a serious violation of a major one may cause a license to be suspended for a period of time, after which it is automatically restored. In some states, however, a major infraction causes revocation of the license, requiring the submission of a new application, after a year's lapse, for reinstatement. I have some friends who maintain driving licenses in two or three states in order to avoid this possibility. This is fairly easy to do, but if you are picked up and show a license from a different state, you are going to have to come up with a good story as to why it is from a different state than your car registration. This could be because you "recently moved."

The Fourth Amendment to the Constitution (part of the Bill of Rights) secures you against unreasonable searches and seizures, and forbids the issuance of warrants except upon probable cause, directed against specific persons and places. Although the automobile was not in existence when that amendment was written, this protection has been extended to the automobile. A policeman can stop your car and prevent you from driving it, but he cannot search your car unless he has reasonable cause. Being stopped for a traffic violation is not reasonable cause. It is none of his business what is in your glove box or trunk, whether it is a radar detector, police scanner, or bottle of booze. A police officer sometimes tries to get around the Fourth Amendment by asking in an authoritative tone if he can see the inside of your trunk. You are likely to say "Yes," thinking he has the right.

The Drinking Driver

What are your rights if you are apprehended drinking while driving? Almost none. You notice I did not say "unfortunately." People driving while intoxicated remain the chief reason pavements are so often smeared with blood and steel. This book was written for the superb driver; the alcohol imbibed in a couple of drinks can move you out of that category. You can find some research that indicates you may be a better driver after one drink. That drink may take the edge off your nervousness or tension by acting as a tranquilizer or sedative. This can be true, but remember, we are talking about one drink. Alcohol is a progressive cerebral depressant. With each successive drink, you lose a little more in reflexes, coordination and judgment, until unconsciousness occurs. The same sequence occurs with several other drugs.

According to the Grand Rapids Study on the effect of alcohol, the following data is accurate:

Blood Alcohol Concentration (BAC) 0.01 to 0.04 percent

This represents between one and four drinks for a 180 pound man. One drink is defined as one ounce of eighty proof alcohol; a twelve ounce bottle of beer; two ounces of twenty percent wine; or three ounces of twelve percent wine. Accident risk low. Some loss of coordination and driving skill. Caution advised.

BAC 0.05 to 0.09 percent

This level is achieved with four to six drinks by the 180 pounder, or three to five drinks by a 140 pound man. The crash risk is doubled at BAC 0.06 percent, and quadrupled at 0.08 percent. Judgment is affected, inhibitions lowered, and reactions impaired.

BAC 0.10 to 0.15 percent

The 180 pounder reaches this level with six to nine drinks, and a 120 pounder with as little as four to six. They are six to seven times more likely to cause an accident.

BAC 0.15 percent and Up

In this range you are twenty-five times more likely to be involved in a crash.

The presumptive level of "legally drunk" is between 0.08 and 0.15 percent blood alcohol concentration, depending on what state you are in. The body burns up alcohol at the rate of 0.015 percent per hour. The use of this figure along with the previous information can be quite useful. If, for example, you were at the BAC level of 0.10, which is both a dangerous driving level and the legally drunk level in some states, simple calculations reveal that it would take you over three hours to burn down to a reasonable safe level of 0.05 percent BAC. Coffee does little more than give you heartburn, but sugar, especially dextrose, does speed alcohol metabolism.

In many states it is not uncommon for the regular booking process for a drunk driver to take up to four hours, since a trooper may be thirty miles from a booking location. However, a new federally funded program initiated a few months ago is attempting to correct this situation. Instead of taking the drunk to jail, the jail is being brought to the drunk. One ton vans equipped with breathalyzers, video recorders, and booking officers are being used by state troopers and county sheriffs as mini-jails. So, you cannot always count on the availability of time to reduce your blood alcohol level.

In my state, statistics reveal that over the last two and a half years alcohol was a contributing factor in sixty percent of all highway fatalities. In fact, seventy-eight percent of the drivers killed on weekend nights had been drinking. Whoever said, "God takes care of drunks" had better take another look.

I have experienced far too much nasty contact with drunks, on and off the highway, to have much sympathy for them. However, there are a few circumstances in which the one drink guy can run afoul of the law. In some states all you need is liquor on your breath for conviction. In Wisconsin, for example, any driver who has been drinking prior to a fatal accident is automatically assumed to have displayed wanton recklessness (rather like the prima facie speed laws I discussed in an earlier chapter) and is charged with voluntary manslaughter, regardless of whether or not he is legally intoxicated. A prison sentence may follow. To guard against this eventuality, I always carry a breath spray in my car and use it whenever I have had a drink.

By the way, if you think the U.S. sentences are rough on drinkers, you ought to drive in Europe. In Italy, if you drive while drunk, you can be fined $108, and sentenced to six months in jail. In Sweden there is a mandatory imprisonment in a "rehabilitation camp." In Denmark, drunk driving costs a month's salary. In Switzerland you can be fined the incredible sum of $16,000!

In most states a suspect does not have to act drunk in order to be charged with driving while intoxicated. Balance tests are often conducted at the roadside by the officer. On the basis of his suspicions, real or imagined, you can be pulled in for a drunkometer test, blood alcohol, or whatever, just because you have had a single drink. True, the tests would come out negative, but you certainly could have your evening destroyed.

In some states, patrolmen collect breath samples in a balloon at the scene, which prevents the time factor from helping you metabolize the alcohol. Up until a few years ago, a driver could refuse such tests on the basis of the Fifth Amendment, which provides that no person shall be compelled to testify against himself. Most states now assume, however, that any driver using a public highway has automatically consented to any tests of his driving fitness. In fact, all states now have chemical test legislation and, except for Illinois, have implied consent laws. Refusal violates the conditions under which the driver was issued a license, and the license can be revoked. The Federal Supreme Court has recently found no constitutional violation in extracting a blood sample from a person suspected of drunken driving, or compelling suspects to provide a voice or handwriting sample.

It would appear that mandatory breath test legislation has been ineffective in deterring drinking drivers, according to a statement released in conjunction with an international conference on traffic safety in Montreal. Figures were produced showing that in three Canadian provinces, drivers killed in traffic accidents with a higher-than-legal blood alcohol level numbered about the same in 1972 as before the mandatory breath testing went into effect in 1969.

Although there are a number of ways to effectively beat a potential drunken driving conviction, I cannot in good conscience offer them.

Non-Moving Violations

This section, something of an afterthought, was triggered by a recent incident, last week, in which one of my good friends was as-

saulted by a flashing, siren-wielding squad car. The cop, who had been in his car crouching in wait, popped out and apprehended my friend. The crime was neither robbery nor rape, that is, not until the officer issued a ten dollar ticket for jaywalking. My friend, an attractive woman, was also subjected to the harassment of an elaborate, "I'm saving your life, you ought to thank me" lecture.

Let us take a critical look at his self-proclaimed "lifesaving." Recent evidence indicates that crosswalks are the most dangerous places to cross streets. During the first few months of 1977, in Seattle, seven pedestrians were killed crossing at intersections, six of them in painted crosswalks. Five of the accidents occurred in broad daylight, when the crosswalks were clearly visible. The city engineers suspect that marked crosswalks provide a false sense of security, since they have documented evidence showing that the number of people killed crossing Seattle streets using crosswalks is five times greater than the number killed at unmarked crossing areas.

This brings to mind an incident with a French taxicab driver. Driving across Paris in the wee hours with minimum traffic, I noticed that the cabby boldly drove through a red light. I asked him why he had ignored it. He gave me an incredulous look. "Monsieur," he explained, "there were no cars coming. I am a human being, endowed with very sophisticated senses. That is merely a small black mechanical box. I should let *it* tell *me* what to do? If there were cars coming and it told me to go, should I go? Of course not. Monsieur, it is simply a convenient arbiter if there is much traffic. Man should not be ruled by machines."

The Frenchman was applying common sense and logic to traffic laws. Unfortunately, little of that attitude exists in the American approach to traffic. Parking is a particularly conspicious example. Since I am more familiar with Seattle than with most other large cities, allow me to use it as an example.

Seattle has a population of about 500,000. On a typical day about 2,000 parking tickets are issued. Last year, close to 521,000 were written, a figure exceeding the number of residents. The lunacy has only just begun to become evident. Seattle has 8,850 parking meters, which pulled in a revenue of $1.8 million in 1976. The overhead for enforcing parking ordinances, including salaries and operating expenses for several agencies (the parking enforcement officers, parts of the Engineering Department, and the Ordinance Violations Department) costs over $3.0 million a year. Thank God for law breakers, or the Violations Department would go bankrupt! They make ends meet by receiving $2.5 million per year in revenues from parking tickets. That is quite a system.

Actually, there are some forty different ways to incur the wrath of the parking ticketeers and find yourself with a parking citation. The violations and current fines (up 100 percent in most charges over a year ago) look something like this:

After seven days you must pay the amount in Column B.

	Column A	Column B
Alley Parking	10.00	15.00
Angle Parking	10.00	15.00
Blocking Driveway	10.00	15.00
Blocking R.R. Tracks	10.00	15.00
Blocking Traffic	20.00	25.00
Bus Zone	15.00	20.00
Tow Away Zone	15.00	20.00
Double Parking	10.00	15.00
Feeding Meter	10.00	15.00
Fire Exit	10.00	15.00
Fire Hydrant	10.00	15.00
Front Wheels not to Curb	5.00	10.00
Hooded Meter	10.00	15.00
Improper Display of License Plate	5.00	10.00
Improper Parking	15.00	20.00
Keys in Ignition	5.00	10.00
Moving Vehicle in same Block	10.00	15.00
Municipal Property	5.00	10.00
No Current License Plate	5.00	10.00
Obedience to Traffic Signs	10.00	15.00
Overtime	3.00	6.00
Parked too close to Stop Sign	10.00	15.00
Parked too close to Crosswalk	5.00	19.00
Parked in Crosswalk	15.00	20.00
Parked in Driveway or Driveway Return	10.00	15.00
Parked on Planting Strip	5.00	10.00
Parked too close to R.R. Crossing	10.00	15.00
Parked over 24 Hours	5.00	10.00
Parked on Sidewalk	10.00	15.00
Parked Wrong Side of Street	8.00	10.00
Parking Certain Vehicles Only	10.00	15.00
Parked in Park	10.00	15.00
Passenger Vehicle in Truck Zone	10.00	15.00
Passenger Zone	10.00	15.00

Peak Hour Parking	15.00	20.00
Prohibited Area	10.00	15.00
Securing Parked Vehicle	20.00	25.00
Stand in Load/Unload Zone	10.00	15.00
Truck Load Zone	10.00	15.00
Wheels over 12 inches from Curb	8.00	10.00

Of course, the fine schedules differ in different cities. These happen to be from Seattle; New York City's are at least fifty percent higher.

Several of these violations are of particular interest. You will notice that you can be ticketed for improperly displaying, or not having, a current license plate, even though you are not operating the vehicle. You can get a ticket for leaving your keys in the ignition. This is to "prevent a good boy from going bad." (You might also consider taking your hub caps with you to promote the same cause). You will notice that if you rush up to your car just in time to get a dime into the meter before it flashes red, you can be ticketed ten dollars for feeding the meter. If you let it starve all day, it would only cost you three dollars. The same goes for moving your car farther down the block to a different spot. Another interesting inequity is the fact that the fine for being parked too close to a railroad crossing is the same as the fine for completely blocking the railroad tracks. I would guess that the potential end product might even this one out.

Some of the violations are not particularly clear; for example, the one listed as "Securing Parked Vehicle." It refers to not turning the wheels in or out and not applying the emergency brake when parked on a grade.

Upon receiving a parking ticket, three options are available to you. One is to pay the ticket, preferably within the specified time limit, to avoid an increased fine. Another course is to secure a court date. This is rarely of value. The procedure involves appearing in person at the traffic violations bureau and requesting a hearing, usually scheduled three weeks to two months hence. Keep in mind that unless there are some extraordinary circumstances, statistics reveal that you have less than a ten percent chance of winning your case in a municipal court. An appeal to the superior court is available, if you have unlimited time, money, and patience.

A broken meter does not require a court date, but does require appearing at the traffic violations bureau, so that someone can document the fact that the meter was out of order on the day you were ticketed. It is not rare to find meters ticking away at a rapid pace, devouring your change more quickly than the allowable time. Again

— even though the system failed, the entire burden is on you to prove your innocence.

Your final option is to ignore the ticket. If you choose this route you can expect a notice from the violations department reminding you about it. This reminder also generally increases the frequently doubled fine to triple. Dunning letters follow, but in Seattle arrest warrants are not issued until the citizen has accumulated three unpaid tickets. At that time a five dollar warrant charge is added, and you join an ongoing fraternity of between twenty and thirty thousand people. If you are living within the city limits, are easy to find, and there are enough law enforcement personnel, you can expect a knock on the door and a free trip to jail. I should add, however, that very few people have actually gone to jail over unpaid parking tickets. A look at the accommodations generally stimulates the paying of the bail.

As you have no doubt perceived, this chapter has not yet told you how to avoid parking tickets. Most of the methods are illegal or chancy, the meters are more annoying than expensive, and the penalties are not ordinarily of sufficient magnitude to warrant a court appearance. Still, a few comments in this regard are in order.

If I have occasion to park in a loading zone or an alley to conduct some limited shopping or errand, I routinely do one or all of the following, depending on the area: 1) Turn on my flashing hazard lights; 2) Leave my trunk open; 3) Place a small business sign in my window. All of these convey the impression that a legitimate stop is being made. I have never been ticketed under these precautionary circumstances.

Timed parking zones without meters are usually monitored by an officer who places a chalked mark on your tire as he notes the time. I know of no law against rubbing chalk smudges off your tires.

Parking tickets received outside your city of residence can ordinarily be ignored. Arrest warrants for parking offenses are not served outside city limits.

There are a great many legal questions concerning parking meter offenses. One of the most basic involves who owns the street. Since it is public domain, and your taxes have already paid for it, is it reasonable to be charged for using it? An interesting question. Another involves accusing a man of a crime and prosecuting him without witnesses and nothing but flimsy circumstantial evidence, unless he confesses. His wife or friends or even a thief may have broken the law. The vehicle cannot commit a misdemeanor. The owner is presumed guilty until he proves himself innocent. This is not consistent with our other legal processes. An additional question has been raised in some cities, where the meter maids are simply city employees. Do they have the legal credentials to issue a ticket?

Most of these issues have not been resolved, and probably will not be, because of the small amounts of money involved. Since the maximum fine is ordinarily less than twenty dollars, incurring no threat to your driving record and license, and no raise in your insurance premiums, how much time and money can you afford to spend launching a court test case? For some people such test cases could be worthwhile, though, because thousands of businessmen park as they please, never pay until caught, and simply count it as a business expense. A Seattle businessman recently paid over a thousand dollars in fines for overtime parking tickets he had accumulated over a three month period.

Incidentally, on two occasions, having received an overtime citation, I tried moving to a new expired meter location to conduct business several blocks away, leaving the ticket in place to indicate that I had already been ticketed. No dice. I just found a ticket twin under the wiper. Meter checkers have specifically assigned territories which remain quite constant through the years. Finding a ticket issued by someone outside their boundaries annoys, but does not fool them.

A year or so ago I came upon my parked car being prepared for impounding by a tow truck. A yellow ticket waved mockingly from the windshield. At that time, in that city, a car could be impounded for any zone violation if the officer in charge saw fit. Apparently he saw fit. I saw red. On an impound, the cop tickets the car and then radios headquarters, which in turn radios or phones a towing company. Since then, a few laws have changed to mandate impounding only if the vehicle is creating or causing a hazard to the public. I told the truck driver to get his hooks off my car. He told me that I would first have to pay him fifteen dollars for his time. I answered that I had made no call to him, and that I intended to have him charged with second degree assault on my motor vehicle, at which he quickly removed his gear and slunk away. I have always thought that it was a particularly innovative charge, but I am glad I did not have to find a statute to uphold my position.

Incidentally, do not think you can avoid the traffic laws by riding a bicycle. In most states, the laws applying to automobiles are also enforced on bicycles. While few citations are issued for speeds over fifty-five miles per hour, I do have a friend who was ticketed on his ten-speed for doing thirty-five miles per hour in a twenty-five zone. I also know someone who got a twenty-five dollar fine for running a stop sign on his bike. I think what really galled him was that the offense was recorded on his official driving record, which placed both his driving license and insurance rates in jeopardy.

Chapter XI
The Insurance Problem

As you may have already painfully discovered, what you do on the highway has a direct influence on your insurance rates. This is true even if you never have an accident or a claim against your insurance carrier. I have often thought that this whole concept is just a shade away from double jeopardy. First, you pay a fine for speeding, presumably clearing your debt to society, and then you pay an increased insurance premium ("second fine") for perhaps two or three years thereafter. While some companies are tougher than others, most *will* increase your rates if you accumulate a few traffic tickets. By and large you get what you pay for. The cheaper the premiums, the tougher the company; in other words, they will increase your rates more readily and cancel you more quickly.

If you expect to gather traffic tickets, you would do well to carefully investigate an insurance company's policy in this regard before buying. If you wait until they cancel or fail to renew you, you will find rates exorbitant when you begin shopping for a new carrier.

In an effort to accumulate useful insurance information relating to traffic tickets, I prepared a list of pertinent questions which I submitted to various carriers. The answers are necessarily a composite of the most prevalent policies.

How do insurance companies receive notification of traffic violations?

They subscribe to a state motor vehicle report that lists violations and violators.

Does the underwriter pay for this service?

Yes.

What violations are received? Only moving violations? Warning tickets?

All violations are received by the insurance companies; that is, violations for defective equipment as well as any moving violation. Warning tickets are not included on the motor vehicle report.

Are out of state and city violations received also?

Out of state violations are included only if the underwriters request a motor vehicle report from that particular state. City police tickets are usually included. Some companies, however, do not attach as much importance to city tickets as they do to state.

How long does it take for the carrier to receive this information?

Normally it takes from ten days to two weeks for the underwriters to receive a motor vehicle report after it has been requested.

Do the violations go just to the particular carrier or to all insurance companies?

The violations go only to the particular carrier that ordered the motor vehicle report.

How do the violations relate to premium increases?

Most companies increase rates as violations are accumulated, a policy somewhat akin to the Point System as used by some states. The degree of increase varies from company to company. A few companies do not relate rate increases to violations.

How long will the rate increase stay in effect? Is the slate ever rubbed clean?

Generally speaking, the greatest increase for a violation will be for the most recent experience year. If an insured is not convicted of a moving violation within a three year period, he is assigned to the lowest rate or preferred risk category. At that time the slate is rubbed clean.

If an accident occurs which is not your fault, will your rates increase?

When it is shown that an insured was not responsible for an accident his rate is not ordinarily increased, but if you accumulate several no fault accident claims against your company, it is likely to increase your rates.

Do liability premiums vary with the type of automobile you drive?

Yes. Regardless of how free your record may be of violations and/ or accidents, you can expect to pay higher premiums if your car has been modified or souped up, even if these changes may provide a greater safety margin. Some companies will not even accept you as a client.

Many of the largest insurance companies have in recent months embarked on a policy of declining insurance on *any* sports car.

Sports car drivers are being forced to seek out those high premium companies which will accept them.

What conditions dictate failure to renew, or cancellation of, your policy?

Numerous moving traffic violations, accidents, or an alcohol problem generally dictates such a move. The conditions vary greatly with different companies, as previously mentioned, and vary from sensible to capricious.

What then?

You will be placed in an insurance pool of poor risks. You will be able to get limited coverage for unlimited rates.

All the above question-answer information points to the necessity of carefully selecting both a good agent and a good carrier. At one time my auto insurance was in the hands of one of the large, widely advertised, cheap companies. At the end of an accident-free, ticket-free year, I was informed that they had made a mistake, and that I owed them more money, because I had received a traffic ticket prior to that year. I explained that the year just past had cost them nothing, and that my premium was merely money in their pocket. Their answer was that even though nothing had happened, something had been more likely to happen, so they wanted more money after the fact. Such is the insurance mentality.

Particularly interesting is the fact that most insurance companies increase your rates, or even cancel your coverage, if you accumulate traffic violations. As a justification, they will tell you that you are more likely to have a fatal accident. Do the statistics support this contention? They do not!

National accident statistics show that in seventy percent of fatality cases, the driver's record revealed no serious driving violations. In eighty percent there had been no previous accident, and eighty percent were driving within the law at the time of the fatal accident. In other words, habitual traffic offenders and accident prone drivers account for just fifteen percent of all accidents.

Another excess profit game played by the insurance companies relates to the ownership of multiple vehicles. Even though you can drive only one at a time, the company will hit you with a full premium on each vehicle, less perhaps a fifteen percent discount.

Two of the largest auto insurance carriers recently announced record profits. One was providing refunds to its customers for the overcharge, as required by a state law. The other, based in a different state, even decided against decreasing premiums, insisting that conditions could eventually change for the worse.

Again - such is the insurance mentality.

Chapter XII
Between Ticket and Trial

Quite a bit of maneuvering and breaching of the bureaucracy must be undertaken between the time you receive your traffic ticket and your actual day in court. The system is designed to discourage court appearances, primarily because of time and government expense. Example: A $5 traffic ticket issued to a Seattle driver had, after one year, cost the taxpayers $1,136, not counting attorney and witness fees, and was on the way to costing much more. The ticket was issued for failing to come to a complete stop for a stop sign. The defendant pleaded not guilty and asked for a jury trial. Remember that in order to arrive at a verdict, all of the jurors must unanimously agree, which, in this case, they were unable to do. It ended in a hung jury, as did the second trial. The breakdown of the $1,136 chalked up in superior court costs goes like this: $896 for salaries of the judge, court clerk, bailiff, and reporter, including heat, lights, and insurance, plus $240 for the twenty-four jurors. The last I heard, the case was still unresolved.

In order to give you some insight into the period this chapter covers, I have chosen a personal experience which includes most of the essential features.

I had been eastbound behind a city bus that was preparing to turn left. The light was green, but the bus did not move because of oncoming traffic. Slowly, I swung around to its right to pass. The centrally dangling traffic light was hidden from view by the bus. The cars perpendicularly to my right were stopped, obviously waiting for the light to change. The bus began to turn left, indicating the light was still green. I started through the intersection. Somewhere past the halfway point I caught a glimpse of the light. It was red. Two blocks later a flashing light in my rearview mirror pulled me over.

"Let's see your license," came the icy command.

"Officer, I couldn't see the light, and . . ."

"Yeah," he interrupted, already writing out the ticket.

"How about the city bus? How come he didn't get a ticket?"

The police officer was not discourteous, just disinterested. He had the same detached courtesy as an executioner. I signed the ticket, and he roared off.

I examined the ticket carefully. The constitution protects the individual against vague charges of wrongdoing; he has a right to be clearly informed of the charge. For instance, if a cop pulls you over for speeding, he must make this fact clear on the ticket. He cannot simply write down, "Violated State Statute Number 246.21 (7)." Since you cannot be expected to understand such a charge, you could have the ticket thrown out of court on constitutional grounds.

I decided to fight this citation - not only because I felt it to be an outrageous injustice, but for the additional reasons that a moving violation would be entered on my driving record, my insurance rates would increase, and I would be fined. There are, in some circumstances, other essential reasons. I recall my wife being issued a ticket after an accident in which her car was rear-ended. Within a few days, she received notice of a large personal damage suit against her for causing whiplash. When she pleaded innocent to the traffic offense and won the case, the plaintiff immediately dropped the damage suit. The teeth had been removed from her suit along with her alleged injuries.

The ticket indicated I was to call the Traffic Bureau in no less than two days and no more than seven. I called six times on the third day, five times on the fourth, and seven times on the fifth, always getting the busy signal. It seemed they had developed one of the world's most inoperable operations. After the seventeenth call, I dialed the operator for assistance, which she readily offered but was unable to give.

"How can I reach that number?"

"Just a moment, sir. I will check to see if there is a party on the line." Several moments, assorted clicks and buzzes later, she informed me that the line was in working order and in use. She suggested that I try later. I explained that I had called seventeen times at various hours over the last three days, and that the whole system smacked faintly of inefficiency.

"Sorry you feel that way, sir."

"Wait. How about if I place a person-to-person call to that number, and then you can keep trying and call me when you have it?"

There was a long cool pause. "Do you know anyone at that number?"

"No, but I can make up a name."

"Sorry, sir. I can't do that."

"OK, thanks for clarifying the hopelessness of the situation."

"Sorry, sir."

I hung up. After dialing continuously for the next fifteen minutes, I got through. The clerk in the Traffic Bureau looked up my ticket and informed me that the bail was twenty-five dollars.

"Would you please put my name on the jury trial calendar?"

Another one of those long cool pauses. I had certainly had a lot of them lately.

"You'll have to come in for that," came the gruff reply.

"Why?"

"Those are the rules. You must be in by tomorrow. That's the deadline."

The next day found me waiting in line at the Traffic Bureau.

I looked around me at my fellow ticketees, then over the countertop at the clerks. I had the feeling that the crooks looked a lot more pleasant than the Traffic Bureau employees. A big sign behind them announced, "Please show courtesy to our clerks. They did not issue the tickets." I wondered if it worked both ways.

I pushed my ticket across the countertop to a stout, husky woman with glasses. She looked like a retired wrestler. I had a hunch her hairdo might be concealing cauliflower ear. She went to a file, came back, and asked for twenty-five dollars.

"I would like a jury trial," I said.

She took in a deep breath and let it out with a sort of hiss between her teeth, simultaneously issuing a disgusted look. Going to a card index, then to the back of the office and back again to the index, she finally announced, "March nineteenth, nine a.m."

"I'm sorry, but I'll be out of the state on that date."

She hissed again, and told me that was the only date possible.

"Look, I'm only going to be gone for four days. How about a date before?"

"Nope."

"Then, how about one after?"

"Nope."

I do not conceal hostility very well. As I stood there, working up a dark, quiet rage, she left to consult with a superior. I was glad. I was not at all sure that I could have won two out of three falls against her. A gentleman appeared, asked when I would be gone, went to the card index, gave me March twenty-second, and left. The woman began typing a large multicopied form between hisses. She gave me a copy and asked, "Do you want to pay now or in court?"

The first thought entering my mind was that she did not seem to understand the legal system, that I was innocent until proven guilty. This was immediately followed by the unnerving thought that maybe she understood it better than I. "In court," I exhaled.

"If you don't show, we'll issue a bench warrant for your arrest," she sneered.

"Thanks a bunch," I answered.

The paper she had given me was a notice of trial date, a big sheet, eight and one half inches wide by over a foot long, with several of the critical statements in red letters. At the top it said, "City of Seattle, plaintiff, vs. Mason, Gene, defendant." The entire city was against me. The odds flashed through my mind as being 525,000 to 1. Elsewhere it referred to me as the "aggrieved party." Webster defines aggrieved as "offended or injured in one's legal rights." I felt that someone had managed to bury a note of sympathy in the document.

I read the section entitled Defendant's Legal Rights. It stated that forfeiture of bail on a traffic violation would be reported to the Director of Motor Vehicles and recorded against my driving record, but that bail forfeiture is never construed as a conviction. The practical distinction escaped me.

Further, it stated that I could plead not guilty and defend in person, or by counsel. It did not say anything about a court appointed attorney, so I immediately saw the need for preparing my defense. After all, for many years I had been exposed to television courtroom dramas, but it occurred to me that my viewing experience was slight in traffic cases, and overweighted in the murder department.

It brought to mind a friend of mine who was sufficiently impressed by the success of some pleas in homicide cases to enter a rather unusual, but certainly creative, plea in a speeding case. He pleaded innocent by reason of temporary insanity! He told the judge that he had been under a great deal of pressure at work and at home, and that he had been suddenly seized with a strange uncontrollable urge to speed. The urge had passed when he was picked up for speeding. I thought it was a brilliant defense, but the judge did not share my enthusiasm. He was found guilty. Apparently it only works in murder cases.

For ten weeks I contemplated my supposed crime and its defense.

I discovered that in most states there are four options for the plea: guilty; guilty with extenuating circumstances; not guilty, and nolo contendere.

With a plea of guilty you waive your constitutional right to a trial, and admit that you committed the alleged offense. A sentence follows, and the offense is duly recorded on your driving record.

A plea of guilty with an explanation of why you broke the law is permissible in traffic court. This explanation can take almost any form, but often will be the kind of excuse I detailed in your relations with the police officer. You might attempt to show that under the circumstances you acted in a more prudent fashion that would be directed by specific adherence to the law. If the judge buys it as being reasonable, he may reduce or suspend your sentence; nevertheless, the offense is still recorded on your driving record.

Only a not guilty plea gives you a chance to keep the blemish off your driving record, and then only if you are found innocent.

Nolo contendere means, "I will not contest it," a plea made famous by Spiro Agnew and his income tax evasion charge. Not all states permit this plea in traffic court. Essentially, it is like pleading guilty, except that the plea cannot be used as evidence in any future trials; for example, civil suits resulting from a traffic accident. Such suits are consequently the only ones in which it would be used.

The morning of the trial was drizzly and laden with gray clouds, as I left home early to return to the scene of the crime. Part of my brilliant defense involved taking Polaroid photographs of the intersection, revealing how the city buses obstruct a view of the stoplight when they turn left. A traffic light on the corner, instead of dangling from the middle of the intersection, would correct the defect and eliminate the potential danger.

I parked near the intersection and got out my wife's old camera. She had loaded it the night before, making the rather ominous comment, "The druggist says the film might be a little old; if it doesn't work he won't charge us." Small consolation, I thought, if I lose the case because of crummy photos.

I focused the camera, snapped the shutter, pushed the series of buttons, pulled out the film, and counted to thirty. The picture was dark brown from the developer, and so were my fingers. I tried it again, counting to forty. The film was unimproved, but the color of my fingers was darker. I tried once more, counting to fifty. Still no picture, fingers even darker. I gave up and drove to the court in the Public Safety Building.

As I entered the courtroom, I noticed two kinds of faces in the spectator benches. Several back rows were occupied by the bright, shining faces of visiting high school students, there to watch justice in action. In the front rows I saw a scattering of the sullen faces of the defendants. I added mine to the sullen group.

We stood as the judge entered the chambers. All was quiet. I had asked for a jury trial, feeling my peers would be more sympathetic than the judge. Looking toward the front of the courtroom, I saw the judge, the bailiff, the clerk, and the city attorney. There was also a bench full of uniformed policemen. If that is the jury, it seems a bit biased, I thought. Actually, they were the officers who had issued the citations, there to give testimony and act as accusers. Well, I'll try it without a jury, I pondered. I'm always allowed an appeal to the State Supreme Court.

The clerk read the list of defendants, who answered mostly from among the sullen faces. Warrants for arrest were issued for the absent.

The first defendant was called forward. The clerk read the charge and swore him in, along with the officer who had ticketed him. The officer presented his case. The defendant presented his defense. The judge presented his guilty verdict, the fine, and referred him to the bailiff.

The next six cases followed suit, with two of them drawing two days in jail in addition to their fines. One woman showed up with an attorney to fight a five dollar parking ticket. After thirty minutes, she too went down in defeat. I was looking for a pattern to help shore up my defense. I found little reassurance in the trend I saw.

The high school students quietly filed out. They had seen enough of justice in action. Although expecting it, I was startled to hear my name called.

I strode forward, briefcase in hand, a Walter Mitty attorney. Actually, the briefcase contained two sandwiches and an apple. I was sure neither of my defense nor of the quality of prison food.

"Are you Gene Mason," the clerk asked.

"Yes."

"You are charged with failure to stop for a red light. How do you plead?"

'Not guilty."

"The officer issuing your citation is not present. Your case is dismissed."

"You mean that's all?"

"Yes."

"What do I do with all this stuff?" I asked, holding in my hand the notice of trial sheet, the citation, and a receipt, and holding in my mind the many wasted man hours, both for them and me.

"Keep them as a souvenir," he answered.

I left the courthouse feeling a bit frustrated by my lost opportunity to play lawyer. Oh, incidentally, the story has a mixed ending. On the way out, they nailed me for thirty-seven dollars worth of old parking tickets my wife had neglected to pay.

What would the procedure be if the officer had been present, and the court had actually judged my case? The best way to gain that kind of knowledge is to pick the brains of a trial lawyer, which is exactly what we will do in the next chapter.

Chapter XIII
Your Day in Court

A. TRY IT YOURSELF AND WHY.

So, despite all of the precautions and techniques we have described, you got a blue slip anyway. Now what? Lawyers are expensive, and for the most part they do not prepare cases like yours until about ten minutes before your trial. You find you have paid $100 or so for some baggy pants lawyer who now sounds like a prosecutor when he tries to convince you to cop a plea. The answer in almost every circumstance is to try the case yourself. You will be better prepared, you will know the facts better, and your lack of knowledge of court procedure, frustrating as it may be to the district attorney and the judge, who have twenty or thirty cases like yours each day to dispose of, will not hurt you. Of course, there are exceptions to this rule. If your driver's license point total puts you in a precarious position, then certainly see a lawyer; if the charge is more than a minor traffic matter, with potential heavy fines or jail sentences riding on the outcome, see a lawyer also. Notice we say "see" a lawyer. This does not necessarily mean "hire" a lawyer, as you may be able to get some darn good advice with a concise office visit, if you will simply arrange your questions to get the information you need in advance of the meeting. It should certainly cut down the fee for such a consultation if you can eliminate making such a meeting a rambling bitch session about how the cop was behaving and the like.

Once you have tried a case yourself, you will probably never want to have a lawyer handle such a matter for you again. As a matter of fact, it can be downright fun; all you need is a little run-through on procedure, and the attitude that you are not going to take this ticket lying down. Also, there is nothing more frustrating to a prosecutor than trying cases against defendants who appear without lawyers. Such people do not know the rules, waste time, confuse the issues, drag out the trial to unnecessary length, and generally make the prosecutor's life a real hell.

Keep in mind that court systems and prosecutors are set up to handle thousands upon thousands of cases just like yours every year, and that lawyers who appear to defend such cases know the pressures and time constraints on everyone present. If your case is a simple one, it is rare that you will find a lawyer who is willing to make the case complex, at least without simultaneously charging you an arm and a leg for the effort. You are better suited than anyone to muck through your own case, and if you unintentionally cause delay, exasperation, tribulations and trials which are frustrating to the prosecutor, he has one easy alternative - he can dismiss your case or give you a deal you cannot refuse. Only one thing is required of you, and that is that you be willing to put forth the time, effort, and energy which may go into representing yourself. Remember that almost any prosecutor will give you a mild reduction in your charge in return for your guilty plea to the reduced offense, such as by reducing speeding ten miles per hour over the limit (a four point offense) to speeding nine miles an hour over the limit (a three point offense). You can obtain this kind of break simply by entering a plea of not guilty and negotiating with the prosecutor to later change your plea to the reduced charge in return for the reduction and dismissal of the more serious higher point penalty charge. This specific reduction in points is what virtually every lawyer does in every minor traffic case for the money you pay him; since they are playing by the rules in the event of a trial, is it not logical that the prosecutor would give you at least as good a deal, knowing that a trial with you representing yourself will probably run two to three times as long as a trial with a lawyer involved? Take advantage of these kinds of circumstances whenever you can.

B. MAKING A "FEDERAL CASE" OUT OF IT.

One of the primary things you need to keep uppermost in your mind during this pre-trial period is that the judicial system is designed to put round pegs in round holes and to handle your case in a mass production fashion, as it handles thousands of other cases. Your object is to make a square peg out of your case, so that it does not fit into any neatly compartmentalized system. The more time your individual case drains from the district attorney, the greater

the pressure on him to resolve it quickly. If he takes one extra hour to handle your case, that is time wasted from preparation for, or the handling of, many other cases, precious time which he cannot recapture. If you have a basically insignificant type of case, he will soon begin to ask himself why he is wasting so much time on such a trivial matter, and at that point the case has turned dramatically in your favor. First and foremost, do not allow your case to be handled in the assembly line style. Start off by asking for a jury trial, not a trial to the court. On petty traffic offenses, this will normally require your posting a jury fee deposit, but that money will be refunded to you, in all likelihood, whether the case proceeds to a jury trial or not. If you are not familiar with the procedure necessary to obtain a jury trial, ask the judge or his clerk when you step to the microphone at your arraignment, so that there is no question whatsoever in your mind. You can be guaranteed that the worst conceivable kind of case for a prosecutor (or that matter for a judge) is a defendant representing himself in a jury trial. A trial before the judge alone without a jury may consume at most a couple of hours. This is a serious imposition on the court's and the prosecutor's time, when the same case tried with a lawyer might last twenty minutes; imagine the additional pressure on the prosecutor when he is faced with the prospect of a day-long trial with a defendant representing himself. That simple fact alone has already increased your chances of obtaining a better break on the charges than you would otherwise expect.

Most criminal cases in which a jury trial has been requested will qualify for a pre-trial conference. Do not overlook the fact that every extra time that your case must be handled by the prosecutor, it becomes a larger burden for him to bear. Therefore, be sure to ask the judge if the normal procedure is to schedule your case for a pre-trial conference, and if so, be sure to request that one be scheduled in your case.

An extremely helpful procedure to follow is to have the police officer who cited you subpoenaed for the pre-trial conference. The officer almost never voluntarily appears at any such conference, trusting that on such a trivial matter the prosecutor will handle it in the normal way. After he has cited you out on the highway, his involvement with the case is over, unless you go to trial, in which event he will appear on the day of trial. The object of all of this is to have him available for consultation with the district attorney at the pre-trial conference, but equally important, it is to make the officer deal with your case as many times as possible also.

Courts keep schedules of the officers who periodically write traffic citations in their jurisdiction, listing several months in advance that officer's days off, nights off, the days the officer is working graveyard shifts and the like. You will find that your trial will be scheduled during a time when the officer is on duty, so that it is not an inconvenience to him, nor does it require him to come in on his day off in order to prosecute your case. This does not hold true, however, for pre-trial conferences, as the officer does not normally appear at such proceedings. Therefore, the odds are quite high that when your case is scheduled for pre-trial conference, if you subpoena the officer, he will either have been working graveyard shift the night before, or it will be one of his days off. The procedure for obtaining a subpoena is quite simple: go to the clerk's office after your arraignment, have a subpoena issued by the clerk (there is no cost for this service), fill out the subpoena, indicating the name of the party and the date and place where he is to appear, and then simply deliver it to the county sheriff, who will serve it for you. There is a slight charge for this service, but it is incidental compared to the benefit which you will derive from the procedure.

At the pre-trial conference, if the officer fails to appear, simply ask for a continuance until such time as he can be ordered by the court to appear, since you did have a subpoena served on him requiring him to be present. Chances are that he will fail to appear, as the subpoena will probably be served on him more than thirty days before his presence is required. Of course, if the officer does appear, then you can have the district attorney confer with him and confirm information which you have given the district attorney about lack of aggravating circumstances and so on, all of which should benefit you in the negotiation of your case.

A very important part of depending yourself is familiarity with pre-trial court procedure. You should be aware that you have a right to file certain motions in court and to have hearings on such motions as may be required. Most states have rules of criminal procedure which govern these pre-trial proceedings, and nearly every compilation of rules allows certain pre-trial discovery of the prosecution's evidence by defense. It is especially important that you read the rule which in virtually every jurisdiction is Rule 16, because it spells out the information which you are entitled to receive if you make a proper demand. This information will include: 1) list of witnesses; 2) results of mechanical or scientific tests; 3) statements by defendant to be used against him at trial, and 4) compliance with applicable federal regulations, for example, licensing of radar by the FCC.

All of the foregoing information is especially important in your preparation of your case. It is important, for example, to know in advance the identities of the witnesses who will testify against you, and thereby to restrict the prosecutor to only those witnesses he lists. Thus if your case requires testimony about the accuracy of radar, you should know in advance who will testify to that information by the list of witnesses provided. If only the arresting officer is listed, then the prosecutor cannot belatedly call a radar technician during your trial. Likewise, the results of any physical or scientific tests are important. If the prosecutor fails to list the radar results on his reply to your motion, then the officer cannot testify to the use of radar in your trial. Further, asking for the summary of any statement made by the defendant which is intended to be used against him at trial is critical, because frequently the officer will belatedly recall (at the point when his case begins to look weak) that you told him that you realized you were speeding. Unless such a statement is contained in the district attorney's response to your motion, the court will not allow such testimony to come in. Also, the Federal Communications Commission requires that domestic uses of radar be licensed, which is easily obtained by law enforcement agencies by merely filing a written application; periodically these licenses expire, however, and occasionally you may be successful in learning of such an expiration. The critical importance of all of these motions is really in the setting of a stage for your own defense, in convincing the prosecutor that you know what you are doing and mean business, that your case is not to be treated lightly, and that it will demand a great deal of effort on his part in order to successfully prosecute you. The only other alternative is to conduct the case in the fashion that nearly everyone else does, that is, to lie back and wait for your trial to occur, which certainly it will, and by simply taking no action to protect yourself, thereby causing the odds of conviction to increase dramatically. Incidentally, failure of the prosecutor to respond to these various motions may well result in a fifth motion, which could be filed immediately before trial: that the district attorney has failed to provide you discovery, and your case should be dismissed because of his failure to comply.

C. HOW TO OBTAIN CONTINUANCES

Try to keep in mind that the goal of obtaining a continuance is twofold: First, to in fact obtain the continuance and, second, to avoid looking as if it was your responsibility. The best way to obtain a continuance is based on need. If you have some pressing personal matter, such as employment, family crisis, or special demands at work, the court will normally grant at least one continuance for such purposes without any major difficulty. The art lies in obtaining continuances and laying the cause of the continuance at the feet of the prosecutor. This can be done in several ways: for example, schedule your pre-trial conference and subpoena the police officer. Thereafter, if it is truly necessary, obtain a continuance of the pre-trial conference at your own request and be certain to ask the court to continue the subpoena for the police officer until the next date for the pre-trial conference, and follow it up with a letter to the prosecutor asking him to remind the police officer of the new date. Just a short note will do. When the new pre-trial conference date rolls around, the odds are about ninety-nine to one that the officer did not get the message, or forgot, or became confused, or the district attorney has some excuse. You are fully protected, because you asked the court to continue the subpoena, which the court did do, and all of the fault for not having the officer present lies with the district attorney's inefficiency. Your only recourse is to point this out to the court and reluctantly indicate that the officer has to be present for the pre-trial conference, therefore necessitating another delay, this time solely due to the prosecutor's foul-up. It may also necessitate a change in your trial date because of the prosecutor's error, which of course you will reluctantly agree to.

Remember that life works in many peculiar ways, and from time to time officers quit the police force, get divorces, are transferred to other parts of the state, or simply move away, all of which would certainly be to your benefit, since the prosecutor would have to dismiss the case against you. Also be aware of the fact that your police officer continues to write other tickets while your case is pending, his recollection of your case becomes dimmer as weeks wear on into months, and the accuracy of his recollection will undoubtedly fade. Certainly he has notes, but so do you, if you have followed earlier suggestions, and this is, of course, the only ticket you have ever received, so certainly the events are fixed indelibly in your mind.

D. DEFENDING YOURSELF — STEP BY STEP HOW TO DO IT.

Well, despite all of the suggestions listed above, you finally find yourself at trial. There is a jury in there, and they are all waiting to see you (or you have chickened out and agreed to try your case before the judge). First, a few tips on selecting a jury:

The court will start off by addressing a few comments to the jury, then the prosecutor will be allowed to ask the prospective jurors a few questions. After he finishes examining the group of jurors, you may inquire of them also. Give the matter some thought the night before and try to decide what kind of person you would like to hear your case. Lawyers who do criminal defense work generally do not like accountants, business persons or loan company personnel. They do like Democrats, guys wearing flashy shirts, people who look as if they have had a few scrapes in their life, women who work for a living, artists, philosopher types and unreligious persons. Make certain the jury understands that you are presumed to be innocent, and that they must find you not guilty unless the prosecutor proves every single element of his case beyond a reasonable doubt.

Now the trial.

The prosecution always is the first to present evidence. Frequently he will start off his case by making a concise introductory statement. Then the prosecutor will start by calling witnesses - if only one, then of course the police officer. After the prosecutor has asked all of the questions he wants to ask of the police officer, it is your turn to cross examine. Reflect a little on the lawyer shows you have seen on television or at the movies. Most everyone has a reasonable idea of how to go about asking questions of a police officer. The important thing to remember is not to give him an opportunity to ramble on and on in response to one of your questions. Ask him questions which must be answered yes or no, such as "Isn't it true that . . ." Do not ask the officer, "Why did you" or "Didn't you say that . . ." since these kinds of questions will not help your case. Focus on the length of time that has occurred since the incident, the number of citations which the officer issued that day, what recollection he has, independent of his notes, about his contact, his ability to see what he claims he saw from where he was, the procedure which he used in clocking you or getting a radar reading on you, and, using the information elsewhere in this outline, try to determine his unfamiliarity with the radar device used; that is, whether he is aware of specific types of problems which might be occurring, and whether he has any knowledge as to how to test the unit for such problems.

Since the object of this entire exercise is to lull the district attorney to sleep with your long and supposedly aimless questioning of the police officer, it will not serve your best interest for us to describe in detail things for you to avoid asking. The premium is on your muddling through by yourself, occasionally asking questions which to a lawyer may seem stupid, but which to you certainly have an important purpose. The result of all this rambling discourse by you will be that the district attorney will slowly but surely begin to tire of making objections, after he realizes that he is only prolonging the misery for himself, since you have no intention of quitting your cross examination early. Therefore, since he is unable to stifle your cross examination, he will see the case concluded much more rapidly if he simply shuts up and allows you to go on, hoping that you will eventually terminate your questioning when you are satisfied with an answer.

The important issue to recall is that among all of the questions you will be asking, you will also periodically slip in a significant zinger which you pick up from this publication, which will, we hope, solidify your defense. For example: after the police officer has testified you are legally entitled to the notes which he prepared (usually on the back of his copy of your ticket), in order to refresh his recollection, if necessary, about this entire transaction. During your cross examination be sure to ask the court to have him produce those notes, so that you can review them to determine if any of his testimony is inconsistent with them. Rarely are these notes inconsistent with his testimony, since he probably read them shortly before the trial commenced; however, you can also use such a fact in supporting your claim of innocence. If there are no inconsistencies between his notes and his testimony, point out why such notes are taken. Obviously, they are taken by the officer in order to help him remember the entire incident when he is at trial. Many of the things which he will have testified to will not be on his notes, since the notes are normally concise summaries of the most significant facts. The factors which he did not write down were therefore either insignificant at the time and not worth noting, which diminishes their significance at trial when pointed out, or the officer is attempting to embellish his story with additional facts, which he now claims to be important, but which were not important at the time. In either instance his testimony is subject to some strong criticism. Simply point out these inconsistencies during cross examination and save your comments for closing argument.

If the police officer starts to testify about some statement or admission which you made during his testimony on direct examination, be sure to immediately object, that is, just as you have seen on television — stand up in the middle of his statement and state to the court that you have several grounds upon which you would like to object to this testimony, and in order to make a cogent argument on these points without prejudicing the jury you would request that the jury be taken out. The jury will then, at the court's decision, be removed from the courtroom, and you can begin to wax eloquent about an extremely limited area of the law, namely, incriminating statements.

Advise the court that you are requesting that the statement be suppressed as evidence because the prosecution has failed to show a proper foundation to admit the statement. Several grounds for such a motion exist:

1. That you were not properly advised of your Miranda rights prior to the statement.

2. That the district attorney has not demonstrated that your statement was voluntary, which showing must be made to the court prior to being made to the jury. Tell the judge that the United States Supreme Court required that such a separate hearing be held before a judge out of the presence of the jury to determine whether your statement was truly voluntary, as in the case of *Jackson v. Denno*. You may very well leave the prosecutor speechless with such an argument coming from an untrained lay person such as yourself. The kicker is you will be right. Ask the judge to dismiss the case because the prosecutor has improperly brought the matter of your statement before the jury, and if the judge refuses to do so, ask then that the statement be suppressed as evidence because of the prosecutor's failure to comply with the law covering such statements.

After this matter is resolved, advise the court that you wish to take up another matter before calling the jury back into the courtroom. You should at this point object to all of the testimony about the use of the radar device, because the prosecution has failed to establish a proper basis for such testimony. The grounds for your motion are that there has been no showing nor even any testimony to the effect that the radar device which was used by the officer to clock you was a properly licensed use of domestic radar as required by the Federal Communications Commission. For your information, such certificates are granted upon incidental application by any law enforcement agency, but absent such a statement of consent to the use of such domestic radar given by the Federal Communications Commission, any domestic use of radar is illegal. Under such circumstances, it must be presumed that the use of radar upon you was illegal until the prosecution can show through testimony that the requirement of the Federal Communications Commission licensing this use has been complied with. By this time the judge should be falling in love with you, as he has rarely seen a practicing attorney prepare a defense so well. If the prosecutor then attempts to call some other witness to testify about the licensing, you can of course object, because this new person has not been provided to you on the list of witnesses which you so intelligently demanded earlier, and which the prosecution begrudgingly complied with. He is, of course, bound to the list of witnesses which he puts on that document, and rarely, if ever, does he have the foresight to list the party who received such consent permission from the Federal Communications Commission.

At the point in which the trial resumes, you can continue your cross examination, using techniques and points illustrated elsewhere in this publication, focusing on the amount of training which the officer received before being sent into the field with this radar device, his knowledge of common areas of malfunction or misinformation, misreading, and the like. As is indicated elsewhere, high tension power lines in the area can affect the reading of radar, as can the size of multiple vehicles in the roadway or an air conditioner in operation in the police cruiser. Vibrations from the transmission of the automobile can also produce such negative readings, if the radar gun is temporarily pointed at the floor. Thunderstorms, short wave radio, bounce, and numerous other defects or natural phenomena all can affect the accuracy of the radar. If the officer is unfamiliar with such potential defects, he is hardly well equipped to testify as to the proper use of the gun.

A portion of the officer's incriminating testimony against you will deal with his having identified you as the driver of the vehicle. Ask the officer to describe what your condition was like on the date of the contact, that is, what clothing you were wearing, how long your hair was, look away from the officer and ask him what color your eyes were on that day, and the like. Any defect or misinformation concerning his identification of you undermines his ability to observe accurately and make proper recollection of the important circumstances.

By doing your homework, you can find the immediately preceding several tickets which the police officer issued on the same day to other individuals besides yourself. You can determine this information by simply checking with the clerk of the court where your citation was filed and asking to be directed to the index system for tracing other citations by the same officer on the same day. The court clerk will provide to you those files upon request, or at least advise you of the procedure to locate the files yourself, and will also provide you a Xerox copy of any such tickets which you request for a nominal fee. With such preparation you can simply ask the officer about earlier citations he issued on the same day, that is to what persons, the descriptions of those persons, the type of offense and the like. The officer will not be likely to have notes of such contacts in his possession, and therefore must give you only his best recollection of the citations. This will operate to effectively test what the officer's independent recollection of the circumstances of your contact were on that day without his having referred to notes about the case. This can be an especially helpful cross examination tool, particularly when you can then remind the officer by citing to him the sequential ticket number immediately preceding yours. By this point in the proceedings the judge should think you are an outstanding trial lawyer in disguise.

Discuss with the officer the location of traffic control devices in the area in his best recollection. You will, of course, have previously reinspected the area and made careful note of the placement of such devices. Check for size and height of the sign, location, distance from obstruction and so on for any such defects or circumstances which may prove to be a significant defense in your case. Inquire about the lane and road markings in the area which again you will have previously noted with particularity by your own examination of the scene. If you have any questions whatsoever about the propriety of the road markings, the size of the sign or potential obstructions, as part of your pre-trial preparation simply go to the Department of Transportation of the city or county where this incident occurred, and ask to review the Uniform Manual on Traffic Control Devices. This text is a standard publication of the federal government and is used in every state and municipality as the standard for marking roadways and passageways, and for size, height, and shape of signs. Any sign which fails to comply with the requirements of this manual will not provide adequate notice of the speed limit or traffic condition warned of, and therefore cannot be a proper basis for establishing the supposed speed limit which you violated.

Ask the officer whether he has any personal knowledge as to who placed the sign at the location in question. He may well have a very good idea, and he may have hearsay information about the placement of the sign, but personal knowledge requires having been physically present and observed the installation. If he does not have personal knowledge of the placement of the sign by the Department of Transportation of the city or county where the offense occurred, ask that his previous testimony as to what the speed limit was be stricken, because there is not an appropriate basis for that testimony as indicated by cross examination. It must, of course, be established that the sign was validly and legitimately placed by the city or county involved, and not placed there by a prankster or community citizen with a Dick Tracy complex. You are slowly driving the district attorney out of his mind.

From time to time during the course of the trial, recesses will occur, for the purpose of the judge having a cigarette, for the court reporter resting her fingers or to let the jury go to the bathroom. During each of these breaks, discuss the prospects of modifying the charge with the district attorney. As the day wears on he will become more and more convinced that the next several weeks could be spent on this case alone, and the negotiation value of your case will be dramatically increased.

SHOULD YOU TESTIFY? HOW TO DECIDE

Rule number one is — do not bother to testify unless you can help yourself. If you honestly believe that you were going like hell twenty miles an hour over the limit, then do not get on the stand and perjure yourself. Unless you are a hardened con, it will show. On the other hand, if you have a legitimate difference of opinion about your speed, feel free to testify. Normally your testimony will be in narrative form, and you can simply describe what occurred on the day in question, and how you know you were not speeding. Describe such things as the conduct of other cars on the highway passing you or going the same speed as you, your familiarity with your car and odometer, having checked it shortly after the ticket in order to determine the accuracy of your speedometer and odometer, how the officer could not have viewed you from the position where he was sitting, despite his testimony, how the officer's radar gun either malfunctioned or did not work properly when he demonstrated it for you, and the other material which you collected in your investigation of the case, both on the scene and afterwards. Be well aware of what the speed limit was, and do not testify unless you can honestly state that there was no violation whatsoever. If you testify that you were going a few miles an hour over the limit, but not as much as the officer contends, you might as well have entered a plea of guilty to a reduced charge several months earlier, because you have just convicted yourself of the lesser offense as a minimum, and perhaps the jury will still convict you of the maximum, if they happen to believe the officer.

Be aware that juries are skeptical of the testimony of a defendant, because they see him as having an ax to grind, and see the officer as simply doing a job, with no interest in the outcome of the case. For this reason, it is important to back up your testimony with corroborating evidence of some kind, and here is where your previous preparation will really pay off. You can describe distances, calculations, time, speed and distance equations and like means, if possible, to show that you could not have been going the speed the officer claims, since you left Joe's Diner at precisely 2:30 p.m., and had you been going the speed the officer claimed, you would have been well past the point where he clocked you. The major point to recall regarding your own testimony is be sure of yourself, be precise, be factual and be accurate, and above all, do not testify unless you can tell the truth. Any intentional shading of your testimony or embellishment beyond the truth will be likely to show to the jury, and will certainly be subject to pointed cross examination by the prosecutor.

PLEA NEGOTIATIONS

Generally speaking, as we have indicated earlier, you can get a mild common reduction of a standard traffic ticket of almost any variety by simply asking for such a reduction, in return for pleading guilty to the reduced charge. We have also given you some indications of the type of disposition which you can obtain by making a negotiating nuisance of yourself, or even perhaps at trial. In meeting the district attorney or the prosecutor handling your case, it is helpful to understand a few additional bits of information beyond those already provided.

1. He is very, very busy, handling thousands of cases like yours every year.

2. He wants to treat your case in the standard fashion and get it disposed of as quickly as possible. He gets paid the same for long trials as he does for dispositions.

3. He probably has at least some rudimentary interest in getting bad drivers off the road, or at least improving their driving habits, and he considers you to be a driving risk.

4. He has no power to determine what points will be assessed for any driving violation, but he does control what offense you will be convicted of, if any, and in that sense controls everything. Therefore, do not be misled by his suggestions that he has nothing to do with the assessments of points. By giving you different plea alternatives, he controls the number of points which the Motor Vehicle Department automatically assesses.

He has probably given many deals better than he will offer you the first time around for the same type of driving conduct. The people who persisted got the better deal.

Occasionally prosecutors like to use a tool called "deferred prosecution" or "deferred sentencing." These procedures have a great deal in common, and essentially operate as follows: The defendant enters a plea of guilty to the charge, his case is placed in a deferred prosecution or deferred sentencing category, which essentially means the conviction is not final; you are then required to drive for the next period of approximately six months without a moving violation of any kind whatsoever. If you do have a subsequent conviction of a moving violation, then the deferred sentencing becomes a final conviction also; if you complete the six months without an additional moving violation conviction, then the deferred sentencing is concluded by your case being dismissed by the prosecutor and no record of your plea of guilty is kept. This can be a particularly helpful alternative in the event that you have serious point problems and could not afford to have any conviction of any kind whatsoever. It is also particularly helpful for young drivers, who are allowed to accumulate only a small number of points compared to adult drivers. One of the best arguments for deferred sentencing is that it makes the driver particularly careful during the time of the deferral, as any moving violation thereafter has doubly serious consequences. If the prosecutor is interested in behavior modification and making you a safer driver, this may be a solution which appeals to him.

CUTTING YOUR LOSSES IF CONVICTED

If the unhappy eventuality occurs that you are convicted of some offense, the circumstances will always occur that you will need to appear before the judge in order to have a fine fixed for your transgression. Most judges who hear traffic matters have heard every explanation under the sun during their tenure, and little you would probably say on your own behalf would be unique. The challenge is, in the face of such circumstances, to truly say something unique. Obviously, if you have a good driving record, and no convictions within the previous year, the judge will probably give you the minimum fine for the offense. As you must undoubtedly know, most judges have strong preconceptions about how to treat certain kinds of cases. Twenty dollar fine for this offense, thirty dollar fine for that offense, fifty dollar fine for a second offense, and so on. As long as you stand silent, your case will become the proverbial round peg in the round hole, and nothing unique about your case will justify or even encourage the judge to do anything other than his normal procedure. Therefore, when the opportunity presents itself, and the judge asks if you have any comment to make, do not pass up the chance. Tell him about your exemplary driving record. Make sure the judge knows that you have lost money by coming to court on these several occasions, which money you will not recover. Make sure the judge knows that this entire court process has been a very rewarding personal experience to you, in watching the court system in operation, and in seeing how courteous and fair the judge is to others who have appeared before him. Judges, as you know, in most states must run for election periodically, and one does not cast away an apparent supporter cavalierly. Persuade the judge that it is the fact of the traffic contact and the fact of the court appearances which have had the important effect on your life, and that any corrective measures which needed to be taken in your driving habits have already occurred because of these experiences (not because of any fine which he might be thinking about giving you). Make sure the judge knows that you took driver's education or traffic school at some time in the recent past, if such is the case. Remind him that your insurance rates will go up because of the conviction, and of any other circumstances of the case which you feel indicate your being a good citizen, such as the officer noting that your attitude was good and cooperative or the like. Do not be so crass as to ask the judge to give you no fine at all, because he does not have the power to let you off scot-free. You should, on the other hand, suggest to the judge that he please take these factors into consideration in determining whether suspension of your fine is appropriate under the circumstances (or at least suspension of part of the fine), and he will be much more likely to be impressed with your presentation. Try to be as sincere as possible in your presentation, or once again an insincere facade may create more problems than standing silent. All judges want to hear the information you are providing, particularly what you have learned from the experience. Traffic judges in particular have a high level of frustration in not being able to modify conduct, and hearing a convicted traffic defendant acknowledge that the experience has benefited him and has resulted in his becoming a more careful driver is music to a judge's ear.

In the same vein, if you feel it is appropriate, you might suggest to the judge that you have not been to traffic school and feel that you would benefit from the opportunity if the court could consider suspending a portion of your fine as a condition. You will need to decide in your own mind whether the likely fine for the level of offense of which you were convicted is intolerable or not, and whether any significant benefit can be derived from attending several night sessions of a traffic school for the kind of a partial fine suspension which the judge might grant. Ultimately, the question is a financial one to be balanced against a time factor, and a decision to be made on the scene by you in your individual circumstances. Be aware, however, that sometimes there is a fee for the traffic school, and you may simply be paying the money into another pocket, rather than saving the money yourself.

MINIMIZING A BAD DRIVING RECORD, MAKING THE MOST OF IT AND FULFILLING THE COURT'S PURPOSE AS WELL

The real danger that most persons facing sentencing on traffic violations have to contend with is a high fine or even worse, a potential jail sentence due to a previous bad driving record. Such persons are looked on by the court as chronic offenders that require particularly strenuous treatment in order to make them pay more attention to their driving. Incidentally, most judges will have a copy of your driving record immediately in front of them at the time of your sentencing, either acquired by the court, or furnished to them by the district attorney. In such circumstances you can only aggravate your situation by denying the facts which are staring the judge in the face, so do not make a liar of yourself to boot. If the judge inquires of your driving record, at least be honest with him. That is perhaps the most important factor to remember, since dishonesty will simply aggravate an already bad situation.

You are in a unique position if you have a bad driving record, because your case will cause the court to try in some way to call your attention to your driving, and the judge will probably be considering the routine way of doing so, namely imposing a heavy fine. Other suggestions may work well also, however, and you should make the judge aware of some of the other alternatives which may exist. Acknowledge your driving difficulties. If you have not been to traffic school for some time, make the court aware that you would like to develop some defensive driving skills. Definitely do not use excuses such as you have a hot car which the cops know well, and they are always looking for you, or variations on that theme. They will not be persuasive with the judge, who has heard the routine many times before. Instead, tell him that you have thought and thought about what you should suggest to him as a way to assist you in correcting your bad driving habits and developing better and more dependable driving skills. Point out that you have come to the conclusion that your real difficulty is inattentiveness, that is, that you let the speedometer creep up past the speed limit, without actually intending to speed, that you are careless, that you do not pay sufficient attention to road signs, roadway markings, stop signs, traffic control devices and the like. Tell the court that you believe that what needs to be done in order to make you personally a safer driver is to somehow make your every driving activity subject to closer attention. Point out to the judge that you have been before courts numerous times in the past, and that each time you have received fines, and that since this is after the fact of the driving violations, it has truthfully had little effect in modifying your driving habits; and the one thing you want to be sure of is that this traffic violation is the last one which you will ever receive.

By this point the judge should have some impression that you have given the matter serious consideration, and we hope he will be interested in your presentation from this point forward.

Tell the judge that you believe the best way to make you a better and more attentive driver is to have a potentially greater consequence for driving errors than just the fine and the points assessed. Suggest that he suspend a significant portion of the substantial fine which you, from previous experience, anticipate he is likely to impose on you, on the condition that you receive no further traffic violations for the next period of four months (or so). Tell the judge that you believe that might accomplish the court's purpose of trying to make you a better driver, and of course if you then subsequently incur an additional violation for which you are convicted, you will have not only that violation, but the suspended fine to pay in addition. Since your real problem is inattentive driving, you believe that making more ride on the outcome of any carelessness or inattentiveness may make you a more attentive driver, and after all, that is what you understand all of these proceedings are about.

Sometimes this approach works exceptionally well, sometimes it falls flat on its face, but at least it is a unique approach which should be tried, since at this point probably nothing else will work, short of moving to another state.

Chapter XIV
Speed Without Fear

A wise author once summed up the writing of a book by saying, "Tell them what you're going to tell them, tell them, then tell them what you told them." In keeping with that sage philosophy, I will offer a brief summary chapter.

Drivers are receiving something in excess of one and a half tickets for every 100,000 miles they drive. Many of you will remember when the usual fine for speeding was a basic amount plus one dollar per mile per hour over the speed limit. We fear that inflation has forever wiped out that standard. While there are considerable variations in fines around the U.S., one of the representative systems goes like this: there is a twenty-five dollar charge for the first ten miles over the legal fifty-five mile per hour limit, and then two dollars per mile per hour for the next five miles per hour over. In other words, you would get tagged thirty-five dollars for seventy miles per hour. From there on, watch out. The fines escalate, and you will qualify for reckless driving in some states past a certain arbitrary speed. This produces an estimated total U.S. revenue of close to a billion dollars a year.

There are ten points which, if followed, can reduce your ticket taxes to nearly zero. Each of these points is, of course, contingent on, and sometimes modified by, a deeper knowledge of the material poured out through the rest of the book.

1. Try not to be conspicious on the road, either through your vehicle or your manner of driving.

2. Always be aware of who or what is behind you. You must be able to identify Smokey and his methods.

3. Be cautious in the presence of white highway marks. They may indicate an aircraft or VASCAR trap.

4. Have a feel for highway traffic flow. Are there groups of vehicles slowing ahead or behind you? Are certain vehicles going especially fast or slowly?

5. Be suspicious of vehicles parked on the median or along the roadside.

6. If your rear is clear, do not worry about closing rapidly on cars directly in front of you. They are running radar interference for you.

7. Buy and use a radar detector. It is essential for the avoidance of over-the-hill and around-the-curve traps.

8. If you are equipped with CB radio, do not be lulled by negative smoke reports, but do pay close attention to positive ones.

9. If you are stopped by the police, treat the officer courteously; it may occasionally spare you from a ticket.

10. If you are ticketed, be sure you know the charge and the precise details of the timing, tracking, radar, or whatever. It might allow you a better day in court.

Would it surprise you if I told you there were warrants out for my arrest in three states? Sounds frightening, does it not? It is not. They are for failure to pay either parking tickets or speeding tickets. I make a practice of never paying parking tickets received in cities other than my own. Expect some beastly letters for a while, and finally a warrant issued for your arrest. The truth is that attempts to serve warrants for parking offenses outside cities in which they occurred has not received much court endorsement.

As far as speeding tickets go, I never pay them outside my state of residence. When stopped it is essential to be a nice guy, otherwise the cop will take you in, and a J.P. will make you pay it on the spot. Convince the officer that you will mail it in. These arrangements are ordinarily available for out-of-state speeders. If you do mail in the bail and forfeit it, many states will reward you by sending a copy of the citation to your home state to be placed on your driving record.

What happens if you do not pay it? You will get a series of dunning letters and threats, and finally a notice of an arrest warrant issued. Well, my most recent warrant came out of sunny California. Snowy, wet weather is here, I have a little free time, and if they want to pay my extradition expenses to that warm clime to pay a traffic fine, I stand ready to go. "Smokey, where are you when I need you?"

Appendix

FCC CB Regulations

The pertinent government regulatory information applicable to various aspects of citizen radio operation is contained in Volume VI of the *Federal Communications Commission Rules and Regulations*. Part 15 pertains to CB operation of extremely low power transmitters (most automobile sets). Part 95 contains the information for the remainder of CB operation. Part 97 pertains to amateur radio operation. Copies of any of these parts can be obtained by writing to the Superintendent of Documents, Government Printing Office, Washington, D.C. 20402, but they do not make for very interesting reading. In an effort to extract the meat, I have summarized the essential passages.

License

In July 1976 the FCC ordered all manufacturers to include a copy of Part 95, a temporary permit (good for sixty days), and an application for a permanent license (Form 505), in all boxes containing CB transceivers.

Effective on January 1, 1977 the FCC began issuing CB licenses at no cost. The permanent license is good for five years. It is illegal to operate without a license.

Equipment

All CB transceivers must be "type accepted," that is, they must carry a label certifying that they meet FCC standards. Any modification to the equipment after manufacture voids the type acceptance.

Only a licensed commercial operator should adjust or perform maintenance on your equipment. Frequency, power, and modulation measurements should be made at regular intervals by such an operator.

Channels

There are a total of forty CB channels available. The use of Channel 9 is reserved for communications involving immediate or potential emergency situations, including assistance to motorists. It is recommended that CB'ers avoid the use of channels immediately adjacent to 9, in order to avoid possible bleed-over interference. Channel 11 is intended as a calling channel only. After establishing contact with another station, you are expected to change to another channel.

Consequently, Channels 8, 9, 10 and 11 are eliminated for personal or business communication. All other channels may be used.

Identification

Radio transmissions should be initiated and ended with your FCC assigned call sign. "Handles" may be used, but only accompanied by your FCC call sign. It is unnecessary to transmit the call sign of the station you are calling.

An identification card indicating your call sign, name, and address should be attached to your transmitter.

Duration of Communication

Because of the enormous amount of radio traffic on CB Channels, CB'ers are asked to limit their conversations to five continuous minutes, to be followed by a silent period of at least one minute.

No-Nos

A citizen's band radio station shall not be used for communicating:
. . . any illegal activity.
. . . obscene or profane language.
. . . music, whistling, sound effects, or inanities.
. . . advertising or soliciting.
. . . Mayday or distress signals unless valid.
. . . to intentionally interfere with another station.
. . . with an amateur radio station.
. . . with an unlicensed station.
. . . with a foreign station.
. . . with a station more than 150 miles away.
. . . false or deceptive transmissions.
. . . a call sign not assigned to his station.

CB Lingo Glossary

CB lingo has become a language in itself, and it is necessary to have a working knowledge of the terms in order to understand the police warnings passed back and forth between the truckers and the other CB'ers. Truckers originated most of this elaborate phraseology to communicate with each other over a wide range of subjects, concerns, and situations. Only certain elements of these conversations are important to us. We must know about police activity, terms related to speed, and jargon that pinpoints the location of the black and whites. For this reason I have included the essential terminology first. The last section of lingo is provided primarily for general interest.

Lingo Related to Police Activity

Advertising - police car with flashing lights in operation.

Back door - the radio-equipped last vehicle in a convoy on the look-out for patrol cars overtaking the convoy.

Bagging - police stopping vehicles exceeding the speed limit.

Bear - police officer.

Bear bait - any vehicle or individual in obvious violation of the law.

Bear bite - speeding ticket.

Bear cage - police station.

Bear cave - police station.

Bear food - any vehicle or individual in obvious violation of the law.

Bear hug - the employment by police officers of handcuffs or physical abuse.

Bear in the air - police aircraft.

Bear in the sky - police aircraft.

Bear lair - police station.

Bear meat - any vehicle or individual in obvious violation of the law.

Beat the bushes - drive ahead of a group or convoy, slightly exceeding the speed limit, to lure police into view.

Big brother - police.

Bird-doggin' - closely following a truck or other large vehicle to avoid police radar traps.

Bit by the bear - received a traffic ticket.

Bit on the britches - received a traffic ticket.

Black and whites - police.

Boogie man - state police.

Brown bag - an unmarked police car.

Brown wrapper - an unmarked police car.

Brush your teeth and comb your hair - radar unit ahead.

Bubble machine - flashing lights on a police car.

Camera - police radar unit.

Catch car - the pursuit car in a police radar setup.

Chase car - the pursuit car in a police radar setup.

Christmas card - speeding ticket.

City kitty - town police.

Clean - no police in sight.

Country Joe - country police.

County mounty - county police or sheriff.

County mounty bounty - a traffic offense fine that is levied at the scene or in the home of a justice of the peace.

Coupon - speeding ticket.

Cruiser - police car.

Dummy - unoccupied police car.

DX - distance.

Electric teeth - radar.

Evel knievel - motorcycle cop, or simply a motorcycle rider.

Eye in the sky - police aircraft.

Feed the bears - receive a speeding ticket.

Fly in the sky - police aircraft.

Foot in the carburetor - police are in pursuit.

Front door - lead vehicle in a radio convoy, usually on the lookout for police activity.

Fuzz - police.

Girlie bear - policewoman.

Good shot - no police or other hazards ahead.

Grab bagging - policeman issuing tickets at a speed trap.

Grass - the median strip separating the lanes of a highway.

Green - the median strip separating the lanes of a highway.

Green stamps - money for speeding tickets, or simply money.

Hiding in the grass - police car on median strip.

Hound men - policemen looking for CB'ers using radio transmitters while mobile.

Invitations - police tickets.

Kodak - radar unit.

Kodiak with a kodak - police with radar.

Lady bear - policewoman.

Lay it to the floor - accelerate.

Little bear - local policeman.

Local constabulary - small town police.

Local yokel - city policeman.

Long arm - police.

Mama bear - policewoman.

Man - policeman.

Mounty - county police or sheriff.

Movie camera - moving radar unit.

Movies - radar readout from a moving radar unit.

Nightcrawlers - many police in the area.

Open season - many police in the area.

Paper - traffic ticket.

Paper hanger - policeman issuing a speeding ticket.

Picture box - radar set.

Picture taker - police using radar.

Pig - policeman.

Pigeon - vehicle stopped for speeding.

Pigeon plucker - policeman who is ticketing speeders.

Plain wrapper - unmarked police car. The usual designation describes the color of the car: for example, plain brown wrapper, plain green wrapper, etc.

Plucking chickens - police issuing tickets, usually at a speed trap.

Politz-eye - police.

Porky bear - policeman.

Rocking chair - the middle position in a convoy between the front door and the back door.

Sandbagging - police issuing tickets, usually at a speed trap.

Shake the trees and rake the leaves - lead vehicle watches ahead for police activity while the rear vehicle watches behind.

Sitting under the leaves - concealed police car.

Smile and comb your hair - radar unit ahead.

Smoke report - location of police.

Smokey - police.

Smokey the bear - state police.

Smokey dozing - police in stopped car.

Smokey on Rubber - police in moving car.

Smokey on the ground - police outside of car.

Smokey's got ears - police with CB radio.

spreading the greens - police issuing speeding tickets.

Spy in the sky - police aircraft.

Teddy bear - police.

The Man - any official or executive.

T.H.E. Man - police.

Tiajuana taxi - police car with the usual lights and identification markings.

Wall to wall bears - many police in the area.

X-Ray machine - police radar unit.

Lingo Related to Speed

Back down - slow down.

Back off the hammer - slow down.

Blew my door off - passed me rapidly.

Dead pedal - slow moving vehicle.

Doing the five-five - moving at fifty-five miles per hour.

Double fever - fifty-five miles per hour.

Double fives - fifty-five miles per hour.

Double nickel - fifty-five miles per hour.

Drop the hammer - accelerate.

Fives - fifty-five miles per hour.

Fives — a pair - fifty-five miles per hour.

Flaps down - slow down.

Got his shoes on - maximum speed.

Got my foot in it - accelerating.
Hammer - accelerator pedal.
Hammer down - speed up.
Hammer off - slow down.
Hammer on - accelerate.
Hammer up - slow down.
Harvey Wallbanger - reckless driver.
Knock the slack out - accelerate.
Lay it to the floor - accelerate.
On the peg - doing the speed limit.
Pushing it - driving fast.
Roger Ramjet - driver exceeding the speed limit.
Rolling road block - vehicle going under the speed limit.
Shoveling coal - accelerating.
Sightseers - slow moving cars.

Lingo Related to Road Geography
Bean store - restaurant.
Boulevard - highway or expressway.
Chicken coop - weight station.
Eat'em up - restaurant.
Fifty dollar lane - left, or passing lane.
Flat waver taxi - highway repair truck.
Four-lane parking lot - interstate highway, particularly when crowded.
Grass - median strip or alongside the road.
Green stamp lane - left, or passing lane.
Green stamp road - toll road.
Haircut palace - overpass or bridge with little clearance.
Hole in the wall - tunnel.
Mile marker - milepost on interstate highways.
Mix-master - highway cloverleaf.
Monfort - passing lane.
Monster lane - inside or passing lane.
Nap trap - rest area or motel.
Oasis - truckstop.
Piggy bank - toll booth.
Post - milepost on interstate highway.
Sidedoor - left, or passing lane.
Super slab - major highway.
Town - any city, regardless of size.
Twister - highway interchange.
Water hole - truckstop.

Miscellaneous Lingo

Anchored modulator- operating from a base or field station.
Anklebiter - young child.
Apple - a CB enthusiast.
Armchair copy - strongly received signal.
Back - back to you.
Back out - stop transmitting.
Bad scene - a crowded channel.
Backslide - return trip.
Backstroke - return trip.
Balls-out - an extreme effort.
Bang a U-ee - make a U turn.
Barefoot - operating without an add-on RF amplifier.
Barley pop - beer.
Barn - garage.
Basement - Channel 1.
Bay City - San Francisco.
Bean Town - Boston.
Beaver - female.
Be bop - radio control signals.
Beer City - Milwaukee.
Bending my windows - strongly received signal.
Big A - Amarillo or Atlanta.
Big D - Dallas.
Big M - Memphis.
Big skip land - heaven.
Big switch - switch that turns off CB set.
Big T - Tucson.
Bikini state - Florida.
Bleeding - interference from another channel.
Blinkin' winkin' - school bus.
Blood box - ambulance.
Bottle popper - beverage truck.
Break - request to communicate on channel.
Breaker - station requesting the use of a channel.
Brown bottles - beer.
Bubble trouble - tire problem.
Bucket mouth - excessive talker.
Bull rack - vehicle transporting animals.
Bushel - 1,000 pounds.
Chain gang - members of a CB club.
Channel 25 - the telephone.

Charlie - the FCC (also Cousin Charlie and Uncle Charlie; affirmative, in some parts of the U.S.)

Checking my eyelids for pin holes - growing sleepy.

Chicken inspector - weigh station inspector.

Choo Choo Town - Chattanooga.

Cigar City - Tampa.

Circle City - Indianapolis.

Clear - leaving the air.

Coke stop - rest room.

Come back - one more transmission.

Copying the mail - eavesdropping on other stations.

Country Cadillac - tractor trailer.

Cowboy Cadillac - Ford Ranchero or El Camino

Cow Town - Fort Worth.

Cut loose - turn off the CB set, or change channels.

Cut out - turn off the CB set, or change channels.

Cut some Zs - get some sleep.

Cut the coax - turn off the CB set.

Despair box - box for CB spare parts.

Dig you out - understand.

Do it to it - start transmitting.

Down and gone - ending transmission.

Down and on the side - ending transmission, but continuing to listen.

Draggin' wagon - wrecker.

Dump 'er in - start transmitting.

Ears - a CB radio or the antenna.

Eighteen wheeler - any tractor-trailer.

Eights and other good numbers - best wishes, love and kisses.

Eighty-eights - best wishes, love and kisses.

Everybody is walking the dog - most channels are occupied.

Eyeball - meet in person.

Fat load - overweight load.

Flip-flop - return trip or U turn.

Flipper - return trip.

Fluff stuff - snow.

Foot warmer - illegal amplifier.

Four roger - OK, received.

Four wheeler - automobile.

Fox Charlie Charlie - The FCC.

Foxhunt - FCC officials searching for illegal CB operators.

Friendly Candy Company - The FCC.

Garbage - unintelligible interference or excessive small talk.

Get horizontal - lie down and go to sleep.

Getting out - putting out a good signal.

Go breaker - invitation to speak.

Go-go girls - pigs for market.

Go-juice - fuel.

Good numbers - so long, best regards.

Ground clouds - fog.

Handle - nickname used by a CB operator.

Hang a left - turn left.

Hang a right - turn right.

Hang a U - make a U turn.

Hangies - wires dangling around a radio installation.

Hang it in your ear - go jump in the lake.

Hit me one time - transmit, so I'll know I'm reaching you.

High gear - illegal power amplifier.

Holding on to your mudflaps - followingly closely

Holler - a call by radio.

Home twenty - home location.

Honey wagon - beer truck.

Hot stuff - cup of coffee.

I'm gone - I'm signing off.

In the mud - signal no louder than the inherent channel noise.

Jaw jacking - talking.

Jawboning - talking.

Joy juice - alcohol.

Juicer - drunkard.

Keep the shiny side up and the dirty side down - don't have an accident.

Kenosha Cadillac - any AMC car.

Key - press the button.

Kiddie car - school bus.

Knuckle buster - fight.

Land line - telephone.

Load of postholes - empty truck.

Load of rocks - bricks.

Load of sticks - lumber.

Lollipop - microphone.

Loose board walk - bumpy road.

Magic numbers - so long, see you later.

Mail - any conversation taking place on a monitored channel.

Make a trip - switch to another channel.

Make your mark - transmit, so I can compare your signal strength to that of other stations.

Mayday - distress signal.

"Running Interference"

Meat wagon - ambulance.
Melting the voice coil - receiving an extremely strong signal.
Modulate - talk.
Motion lotion - fuel.
Motor City - Detroit.
Muff - girl.
Muffin - cute girl.
Negative copy - can't hear.
Negatory - no, negative.
One time - short contact.

On the by - standing by and listening.
On the side - standing by and listening.
Other half - husband or wife.
Overmodulating - talking too loud.
Over shoulder - behind or in back of.
Package her up - turning it over to the other station so they can sign off.
Pass the numbers - sign off.
Peanut butter in the ears - operator not listening to his CB
Peanut whistle - low power transmitter.
Pickum-up - pickup truck.
Pit stop - any necessary stop.
Play dead - stand by.
Play in the sandbox - go to the toilet.
Portable barnyard - cattle truck.
Portable parking lot - auto carrier.
Pository - yes, affirmative.

Prescription - FCC rules.
Pregnant roller skate - Volkswagen.
Pull the big one - turn off the CB radio.
Pull the big switch - turn off the CB radio.
Pull the plug - turn off the CB radio.
Rack - bed.

Ragchew - engage in idle conversation.
Raise - to contact someone.
Ratchet jaw - talkative person.
Read - hear.
Read the mail - listen in on a conversation taking place on a channel
Reefer - refrigeration truck.
Rig - CB radio; also truck tractor.
Road jockey - truck driver.
Rock - crystal for CB set.

Rockbound - operating on only one or two channels for lack of necessary crystals.

Roger - OK, message received.

Roger dodger - OK, message received.

Rollerskate - any small or compact car.

Sandbox - toilet.

Sailboat fuel - running empty.

Seatcovers - passengers, particularly female.

Set of doubles - tractor-trailer.

Seventy-three - best regards.

Shakey City - Los Angeles.

Shakeyside - California.

Shim - illegally soup up a transmitter.

Shoot beaver - watch females.

Short short - soon.

Shout - a call by radio.

Sitting by - standing by.

Sitting in the saddle - middle truck of a three vehicle convoy.

Skating rink - slippery road.

Slammer - jail.

Snake den - fire station.

Snore shelf - bed.

Stepped all over you - interfered with you.

Suicide jockey - driver of truck carrying explosives.

Super skate - high performance car.

Ten out - I'm gone.

Thermos bottle - tanker truck.

Threes - best regards.

Threes and eights - best regards, love and kisses.

Ticks - minutes.

Tie the ribbons - end a communications exchange.

Tie can - a CB radio.

Trading stamps - cash.

Truck 'em easy - have a good trip.

Twenty - location.

Twisted pair - telephone.

Two wheeler - motorcycle.

Uncle Charlie - The FCC.

Walking on you - interfering with your signal.

Wallpaper - a card containing the operator's call name, type of equipment, etc.

Wall to wall - receiving a good signal.

Wall to wall and treetop tall - receiving loud and clear.

Wall to wall and walking tall - receiving loud and clear and feeling fine.
Wilco - will comply.
Window washer - rainstorm.
Windy City - Chicago.
Woolly critter - good looking girl.
Work twenty - place of employment.

Police Codes

If you start monitoring police channels, you will find a number of codes in use. These are used both as timesaving, word sparing devices, and also to prevent your understanding their communications. These may take the form of one and two digits, three digits, colors, tens, elevens, or twelves. Unfortunately, there is no uniformity to the system, so different cities and counties within a single state may each have their own system and may even assign different meanings to the same code numbers. For example, out of curiosity I checked the police radio code for "Officer Needs Help" in several different police jurisdictions in my state, thinking that perhaps I could find some uniformity with that emergency code. I quit checking after I turned up 10-99, 10-33, 12-3, 12-40, 510, 777, 10-78, Code 9 and Code 19. Feeling a bit ill over the lack of consistency, I tried "Ambulance Request" and came up with the following code numbers being used in different counties: 11-41, 12-18, 10-48, 10-50, 10-56, 10-38, 10-52, and Code 32.

However, in spite of the ambiguity, since the ten code remains the most commonly used, I have included a version which lists first the most commonly accepted CB meaning (the Official National CB 10-Code), followed by one of the police meanings. Where only one interpretation is used, it indicates that the meaning is generally acceptable to both, or that only one or the other is using the code number. Notice that the first thirteen numbers, those most frequently used in radio transmission, are the same for both groups. The Official National CB 10 Codes are marked with an asterisk.

10-1   Receiving poorly*
10-2   Receiving well*
10-3   Stop transmitting*
10-4   Affirmative, acknowledged*
10-5   Relay message*
10-6   Busy, stand by*
10-7   Out of service, leaving the air*
10-8   In service, accepting calls*

10-9	Repeat*
10-10	Transmission completed, standing by*
10-11	Talking too rapidly*
10-12	Someone is present who prevents my talking freely*
10-13	Advise weather and road conditions*
10-14	Approximate time by the clock
	Escort detail
10-15	We have passenger(s)*
	Enroute to the station with a prisoner
10-16	Make pickup at . . .*
	Pick up prisoner
10-17	Urgent business*
	Pick up papers or package
10-18	Any assignment for us?*
	Remain in service
10-19	Return to the station*
10-20	Present location*
10-21	Call by telephone*
10-22	Make a personal contact with . . .*
	Cancel
10-23	Standby*
10-24	Assignment completed*
10-25	Make radio contact with . . .*
10-26	Disregard last transmission*
	Detaining driver or subject
10-27	I am moving to channel . . .*
	Any return on your subject?
10-28	Identify your station*
	Record check of vehicle or subject
10-29	Time is up*
	Want check of vehicle or subject
10-30	Does not conform to FCC Rules*
	Computer record check for wanted (vehicle, subject, or property)
10-31	Violation on this channel, but no longer occurring
	Give FCC mobile call letters and channel number
10-32	Advisory regarding reception of signal*
10-33	Request emergency radio clearance for high priority message*
10-34	In trouble at this station, need help*
	Request routine radio clearance to run a subject or number
10-35	A matter that cannot be discussed over the radio*
10-36	Time check*

10-37	Send towtruck*
10-38	Ambulance request*
10-39	Message delivered*
	Requested unit is in service and on the air
10-40	Car to car*
	Meet with the officer
10-41	Moved to another channel*
	Meet with unit . . . , on car to car frequenc
10-42	Traffic accident*
	Direct traffic
10-43	Traffic tie-up*
	See if ambulance is needed
10-44	I have a message for you*
	Traffic accident (no details)
10-45	All units using this channel please identify*
	Traffic accident (no injury)
10-46	Assist motorist
	Traffic accident (injury)
10-47	Arriving at the scene
10-48	Clearing from last detail
10-50	Break channel*
	Ambulance request
10-51	Coroner request
10-52	Call your home
10-53	Abandoned vehicle
10-54	Suspicious person or auto
10-59	Convoy or escort needed*
10-60	What is next message number?*
	No record or wants on your subject
10-61	Misdemeanor want on your subject
10-62	Unable to copy, use telephone*
	Felony want on your subject
10-63	Net directed to . . .*
10-64	Net is clear*
10-65	Clear for message*
10-67	All units comply*
10-68	Repeat message*
10-70	Fire in progress*
10-71	Proceed with transmission in sequence*
10-73	Speed trap at . . .*
10-75	You are causing interference*
10-77	Negative contact*
10-79	Report progress of fire*

10-81	Reserve hotel room for . . .*
10-82	Reserve room for . . .*
10-84	My telephone number is . . .*
10-85	My address is . . .*
10-86	What is your address?*
10-87	Meet with the officer
10-88	Advise telephone number of . . .
10-89	Radio repairman needed at . . .*
10-90	I have television interference*
10-91	Talk closer to microphone*
10-92	Your transmitter is out of adjustment*
10-93	Check my frequency on this channel*
10-94	Please give me a long count*
10-95	Transmit dead carrier for five seconds*
10-96	Transmitting from Mobile*
10-97	Arriving at the scene
10-98	Assignment completed*
10-99	Mission completed, all units secure*
	Officer needs help (emergency)
10-100	Nature calls*
10-200	Police needed at . . .*
10-400	Drop dead*

Police Vehicle Codes

Certain codes are directed primarily from the station to the patrol car to indicate the urgency of the mission, or from the car to the station, explaining why they may be temporarily out of radio contact.

Code 1	Acknowledge
Code 2	Urgent, proceed at once (use lights only)
Code 3	Emergency, use lights and siren
Code 4	No further assistance needed
Code 5	No further assistance needed (suspect still outstanding)
Code 6	Out of the car to investigate (give your location)
Code 7	Lunch or coffee break
Code 8	Fire department follow-up call (aid-call or traffic control)
Code 9	Requesting a back-up car
Code 10	Return to your patrol district
Code 20	Notify news media of a newsworthy incident or sigalert
Code 30	Silent alarm
Code 31	Audible alarm
Code 33	Emergency radio clearance (all units and stations stand by)

Phonetic Alphabet Code Words

Letter	Code Word	Alternate Code Word	Police Phonetic Alphabet
A	ADAM	ABLE	ADAM
B	BRAVO	BAKER	BOY
C	CHARLIE		CHARLES
D	DELTA	DOG	DAVID
E	ECHO	EASY	EDWARD
F	FOXTROT	FOX	FRANK
G	GOLF	GEORGE	GEORGE
H	HOTEL	HENRY	HENRY
I	INDIA	IOWA or ITEM	IDA
J	JULIET	JOHN or JIG	JOHN
K	KILO	KING	KING
L	LIMA	LOVE	LINCOLN
M	MARY	MIKE	MARY
N	NOVEMBER	NAN	NORA
O	OSCAR	OBOE	OCEAN
P	PAPA	PETER	PAUL
Q	QUEBEC	QUEEN	QUEEN
R	ROMEO	ROGER	ROBERT
S	SIERRA	SUGAR	SAM
T	TANGO	TARE	TOM
U	UNIFORM	UNCLE	UNION
V	VICTOR		VICTOR
W	WHISKEY	WILLIAM	WILLIAM
X	X-RAY		X-RAY
Y	YANKEE	YOKE	YOUNG
Z	ZULU	ZEBRA	ZEBRA

Q Signals

This sytem of coded sentences predates all the others. Originally developed to be transmitted by Morse code, it was for many years the mainstay verbal shorthand of military and amateur radio.

QRM - interference from other stations.

QRN - interference from natural (e.g. lightning) or manmade (e.g. power poles) sources.

QRP - transmitter of very low power.

QRT - stop transmitting.

QRU - receiving messages directed to me but have nothing to transmit to other stations.

QRV - prepared to take a message.

QRX - standby.

QRX-1 - wait for one minute.

QRZ - what station is trying to call me?

QSB - rapid fading of signals.

QSL - a card containing the operator's call name, type of equipment, etc.

QSO - conversation between stations.

QSY - change to some other channel.

QTH - home station location.

The Point System

Loss or suspension of your license for a minor offense is particularly likely in those states using a point system to penalize habitual violators of traffic rules. A certain number of points is assigned for each violation, and accumulating more points than permitted within a specified period of time costs you your license.

If your state uses this system, and you have several points on your record, do not grab a guilty plea. Use one of the suggestions advised in our legal chapter. Your latest violation might push the total points over the top and topple your license.

Different states have different point systems, some more equitable than others. The California Point System, fairly typical, goes like this:

Any accident in which the department of motor vehicles decides the driver is responsible — one point.

Any conviction involving unsafe operation of a vehicle - one point.

Driving while license is suspended or revoked — two points.

Causing property damage by hit and run — two points.

Drunken driving without injury or property damage — two points.

Reckless driving, whether or not it causes injury or property damage — two points.

The department can revoke or suspend the license of any driver who accumulates four points or more in a twelve month period, or six points or more in a twenty-four month period, or eight points or more in thirty-six months. The driver is given a hearing before any action is taken.

Some states reciprocate with each other by sending a record of your out-of-state offense to your home state; this too can add points.